WHEN LOVE MEETS FEAR

BECOMING Defense-less AND Resource-full

DAVID RICHO

Paulist Press
New York • Mahwah, NJ

Permission has been granted to reprint lyrics from the song "Outside the Wall" by Roger Waters, © 1979 by Pink Floyd Music Publishers Ltd.

Book design by Kathleen Doyle

Cover design by Vitale Communications, Inc.

Library of Congress Cataloging-in-Publication Data

Richo, David, 1940-
    When love meets fear : how to become defense-less and resource-full / David Richo.
        p.   cm.
    ISBN 0-8091-3702-X (alk. paper)
    1. Fear. 2. Love. I. Title.
BF575.F2R46   1997
152.4´6—dc21   96-39729
                                                    CIP

Published by Paulist Press
997 Macarthur Boulevard
Mahwah, New Jersey 07430

Printed and bound in the
United States of America

Be not afeared; the isle is full of noises.

Sounds and sweet airs that give delight and hurt not.

—The Tempest

CONTENTS

PART TWO: TAKING FEAR BY STORM

Introduction

I realized, in recent years, that most of my decisions were in some way fear-based, that most of my problems had a fear component, and that fear had been a silent companion in all my relationships. I guessed that I was not alone. That guess was the origin of this book. This book is for you if you are afraid of—

your love going too far or not far enough

their love not really there for you or too invasive in the way it is shown

being loved too intensely or too hesitantly

love itself in any form you are not in control of

getting close and feeling unappreciated

getting away when a relationship is not working

changing and losing the safety of the status quo

staying when conflicts keep challenging you

leaving when you know it makes sense but you just can't

being left if you don't toe the line

making a commitment

breaking a commitment

letting go and moving on

1

feeling sad, angry, or joyous

feeling unsafe in the company of someone

laughing spontaneously

acting spontaneously

rejection by others if you don't please them

abandonment by a partner who seems distant

engulfment by a partner who clings to you

betrayal by someone you have trusted

humiliation if you do not find a way to save face

your own potential

your darker side

feeling sexual or not feeling sexual

knowing what you want

knowing yourself

knowing your partner

being known by your partner

giving since more might be demanded

receiving since you are not in control of what is given to you

starting or starting over

grieving the past or any loss

being alone

being with someone

seeing someone as he or she is

letting yourself be seen as you are

asking for what you really want

spending, saving, earning, sharing, or wasting money

failing or succeeding

and finally, fear of not having something to fear

so your mind scans your present life situation to

find something to worry about, often in an obsessive way

We all feel afraid every day. Fear makes us start or stop or holds us back from starting or stopping. Fear convinces us not to risk, that is, not to act bravely and creatively. This is not a book on how to stop feeling fear, but rather on how to feel fear *safely*. Since none of us can live our lives completely without fear, it helps to understand fear, how it gets in our way, how it limits and interrupts us, how it serves us, and how to go beyond it, so that it no longer drives or stops us.

Fear is not always negative. For instance, pain and fear have always played a part in initiation ceremonies or threshold experiences. Sometimes the fear you feel before a new task, or as you pass through a rough-edged transition, may be part of the initiatory trial that any hero faces. A hero is, after all, someone who has lived through pain and been transformed by it.

There is a vast difference between unhealthy, neurotic fear and appropriate fear. This book will help you distinguish between the two. In the following chapters we will address neurotic, or inhibiting, fear as the stressful excitement that the ego thrives on. We will explore our compulsiveness, how we keep ourselves afraid, our resistance, defense mechanisms, panic reactions, and the connection between fear and love. Fear is the only obstacle to love. So working through our personal fears is the path to loving and being loved. Letting go of ego is ultimately the same task as letting go of fear and letting love through.

We will also look at some major fears, such as the fear of love and loss, the fear of change, the fear of self-disclosure, the fear of others, the fear of giving and receiving, the fear of comings and goings, and the fear of aloneness. We will discuss the void: the inner sense of total emptiness in which nothing works and we feel helpless in the grip of desolation and desperation. I feared all these things myself in the course of my life—with many currently on the screen—so I share what I have learned with you.

Bravery in any sphere of life is not the same as having no fear. Physical fears challenge the mind and body; psychological fears challenge the heart and soul. A war hero who showed himself brave in every battle and has medals to prove he really is courageous may secretly have as many paralyzing fears within himself as he has medals. As a soldier, he is a full-fledged adult. When it comes to making a commitment to intimacy, he may be more like a scared child. A woman may say to herself, "I found a real man. This guy is not afraid of anything!" And yet she may not know until she asks for the kind of closeness she wants that he is deathly afraid of his feelings.

Fear of intimacy in one partner is often about both partners. In one way or another, the fear will impact both, impinge upon both, somehow affect both. The partner you describe as "cold" is actually afraid of closeness. ("Cold" means fear in this context.) You feel frustrated and wish he could transcend this fear. But if you are choosing to stay with a partner who fears closeness, does that not mean that you are willing to be in a relationship where there is very little closeness? Could it be that you fear closeness too? He fears closeness directly; you may fear it obliquely through him. Did you look for somebody with this fear so that you would not have to be close either? Only your insistence on change is evidence of a different choice on your part. Since change in a relationship can happen only if both partners commit to it, the challenge is to work together toward safety in closeness.

Most of us have heard about the "inner child," the wounded child of the past in each of us who did not have his or her needs met. There is a "scared child" within us too, the progeny of a scared parent. A parent may look to a child like an adult in control, but inside that controlling adult may be a scared child. In childhood, sometimes we were parented by the scared-child part of our parents, and sometimes we were parented by the empowering, nurturing adult part. All of us have encountered this paradox in our parents, but since both parts looked the same, we may never have articulated it quite this way. Now we understand and can feel compassion too.

This all sounds very serious. Seriousness, like fear, is another word for pain. Voltaire says, "God is a comedian playing to an audience that is afraid to laugh." A simple way to tell exactly what you fear is whatever you just can't seem to laugh about. Humor frees you from the grip of fear so that you are no longer controlled by it. Then you recover your lively energy, that is, your ever-accessible enthusiasm, free speech, and irrepressible delight.

Ask yourself, "Can I see the humor in what I am afraid of? Can I see the humor in my being afraid of this? Can I laugh at myself?" It is not ridicule, but amusement. To paraphrase Maslow describing the self-actualized person, "Finally, you will see everything that happens in life with acceptance and amusement." Humor happens when you believe, incontrovertibly, that you belong here and that everything that happens to you is the legitimate landscape of your path. In fact, fear becomes fearlessness when you see it as part of your path rather than an obstruction on it.

Handling fear takes psychological work and spiritual practice. The work comes from the effort of our healthy ego. The spiritual practice is mindfulness, attention to the breath of reality rather than the gasps of our neurotic and frightened ego. In both instances, we take conscious steps, and graces follow as shifts in our consciousness. There is a Tibetan image for this marriage of effort and grace: the "windhorse." Despite the force of the wind, you remain stably in the saddle. Both the wind and the horse help you move through space; the wind pushes you; the horse carries you. The wind is moving you, helping you go on. The visible support is the horse: your functional ego, the wise people that have helped you, the little choices you make that help you live your life more serenely, the effort you make to live out your program of handling fear, this book! These efforts are often given the boost of grace, an invisible support that takes you beyond what you have the power to do when the scared ego is in the saddle.

Fear lifts more easily when we receive permission to let go of it. You may choose to read aloud any sections of this book that strike you as personally relevant. You may choose to read it onto a tape and listen to it in your own voice. You may want to make affirmations of the statements that most appeal to you. You may faithfully follow the "To Do" recommendations at the end of each chapter, as well as the suggestions within the chapters. These are all ways of making this not just a book to read but *a program of change*. Your transition from fear to love will happen in direct proportion to the work you put into this project.

At the same time, grace builds on effort and often goes beyond it too. Be prepared for synchronicities (meaningful coincidences), relevant dreams, and events in life that season, challenge, and further your commitment to let go of fear in favor of love. Ultimately, fear is irrelevant if you have a program for dealing with it. This book is meant to provide just such a program.

Some themes enter the book again and again but each time with a richer spin, as your continuing reading and working with the ideas make you ready for a deeper grasp of them. These themes are ego, grief, early life, and spirituality. We will see how these four poignant conundrums of our human existence are also the subjects of this book—and of fear itself.

Finally, the underlying theme of this book is non-violence, which happens when we become both defense-less and resource-full. This is the winning combination for freedom from fear. You will find yourself changing in more than one way: less fear, more love…less ego possessiveness, more compassion…less self-seeking, more generosity…and most of all, less belief that you have to do it all and more joy at noticing that doors are opening without your having to push.

This book is written in a conversational way, using "I" and "you" and "we." I am initiating a dialogue with you in these pages. I address myself to you directly. I am dedicating my words to your freedom from fear so that more enlightenment may happen and love may flourish in this miraculous world.

Just a little progress is freedom from fear.—*Bhagavad Gita*

> *Fear is the mind killer. Fear is the little death that brings total obliteration. I will face my fear. I will permit it to pass over me and through me. And when it has gone past me I will turn to see fear's path. Where the fear has gone there will be nothing. Only I will remain.*
> —*Dune:* Frank Herbert

Part One:

Calling FEAR

by Name

1.

How Fear Works

FEAR AND THE CONDITIONS OF EXISTENCE

The law of life lives in the hero with his unreserved consent.

—Mircea Eliade

Our major fears are the fear of loss and change, i.e., letting go and going on, the fear of self-disclosure, the fear of other people, the fear of others' feelings, the fear of rejection, the fear of giving and receiving, the fear of comings and goings, and the fear of aloneness which includes the fear of the void. These are also the ordinary conditions of human living!

Here are four of the main givens of life:

We are ultimately alone;
things are transitory;
life is unpredictable and often unfair;
and suffering seems to be a universal experience.

We may compare the adult response to each given with the response of the scared child. When an adult confronts aloneness, she looks for support and/or stays with the sense of aloneness. This staying is a form of mindfulness: meditative witnessing of the present predicament without judgment, attachment, fear, or desire. The scared child feels judged by aloneness: "This means no one wants to be with me. This means I will die of isolation." I look for a way to fill up the aloneness so I will never have to feel it fully. I am not just looking for someone to support me, I am looking for someone who will take away that sense of loneliness and fill my emptiness. I do not believe I can do this for myself. (Recall that in our humorous path through fear, we take the quotation of the scared child above and say it aloud till we laugh!)

Regarding the transitory nature of things, the adult notices and accepts that everything in life goes through stages. Things rise, crest, and decline and that bell-shaped curve seems to characterize all our experiences in life. When we operate from childish fear, we attempt to fixate or hold on to "what is" so that it will not change, but continually crest. "I have experienced romance with you and now the thrill is gone so I will look for it with somebody else. I do not want to accept that it is normal to go from romance to conflict to mature commitment." This is the Faustian mortal error: "Abide, thou art so fair!"

When the conditions of existence happen with my unreserved consent, I allow things to be unpredictable, sometimes beyond my control. From the perspective of childish fear, I might demand certitude and look for a safe harbor. I try to find something that I can hang onto or hold onto: a person, religion, a guru, a belief system, or an addiction. I feel safe when everything is reliably taken care of and under control. The adult who lives through fear comes to terms with unpredictability and does not try to find a way around it. "Some things happen according to my plan and other things happen contrary to plan. I assent to this as a fact of life." Such assent confers the power to handle unpredictability. This is the paradox: what I accept strengthens me to handle what requires acceptance, i.e., the things I cannot change. In fact, this condition of existence is stated simply as: there are some things I can change and other things I cannot change and that is all right with me—instead of all fight with me!

Another condition of existence is that things are not always fair. The evil sometimes prosper and the good sometimes suffer. There is no one making sure everything comes out justly in human affairs. The scared child wants the predictability of justly imposed verdicts. His presumption is that an all-knowing Judge is meting out justice, punishing the wicked, and rewarding the innocent. A simplistic belief in karma is a form of this. The reality of our observation seems, however, to be quite different or, rather, indifferent!

Suffering is universal. Bad things happen to good people and good things happen to bad people and vice versa. It is unpredictable. The childish wish is that corrupt persons be hurt (punished) rather than reformed or transformed. This emanates from the vengeful ego rather than the compassionate self.

It also seems that suffering in the form of hurt and betrayal in human relationships gives us character. All the people who brought pain to us somehow were participating in what needed to happen for us to grow. Once you see it that way, you realize they were all playing their parts—for better or for worse—and you can finally forgive them. It is appropriate to be angry and resentful, but ultimately then to forgive and see that it all fit with what needed to happen. Nietzsche says: "It took just such evil and painful things for the great emancipation to occur."

A fig tree produces one perfect fig at the beginning of the season. The purpose of this "explorer" fig is to sniff out the atmosphere and to give a signal to the rest of the figs to bloom or not. The signal might be: "Come out," or "It is dangerous out here, too much pollution; do not come out." The other nascent figs receive this message and respond accordingly. Their response to the explorer fig's message is taken without the slightest sense of pain, disappointment, anger, or fear. The message is a pure fact. This is an example of an agreement with reality without protest.

Here is another example from nature (which says Yes and only Yes unconditionally every moment of every century). Before mating, falcons fly close to the ground and scan their whole territory. They count the number of ground squirrels, little birds, and mammals to see whether there are enough to support both them and their young. If there is enough sustenance in their territory, they mate and the female lays her eggs. If the count does not tally, they skip mating for that year. (Imagine how world population figures would change if people did that same thing!) This is done without anger or protest; it is simply matter of fact.

To look at all the conditions of existence and let them land in a matter-of-fact way is mindfulness, full consent to the conditions of existence, without fear or desire. It is settling out of court with the conditions of existence.

A smoker sees the statement from the Surgeon General and says: "Cigarettes are dangerous to my health!" He throws the package into the trash and never smokes again. Without protest, without anger, he is simply responding in an adult way to the information. This is being responsive to what is and honoring it. *Where does information land in us? Does it land on adult soil or on childish rationalization, protest, and demands for exemption?*

The role of faith may arise as a question here. Adult faith happens in the paradoxical gap that opens in us when confronted with the apparent arbitrariness of nature and history *and* the revelation of a providential God. The two facts—arbitrariness and providence—seem irreconcilable but the combining word *and* closes the gap. Simultaneously, we are held and we are not held; we are both at the mercy of circumstance and in the grace of circumstance. Faith never expunges or simplifies our human story. It enriches it by the paradox of simultaneity, the combination of opposites. Nature is unpredictable and all of nature is moving toward an omega point of coherence. Faith accommodates both where logic sees only an either...or.

> *We are wound with mercies round and round.*
> —Gerard Manley Hopkins.

FEAR OF GRIEF

We must in tears unwind a love knit up in many years.
—Henry King

The conditions of human existence often result in pain and loss. Throughout this book, we will see how grief is the healthy human way of dealing with loss. We often fear letting go of what has gone and moving on to what comes next. All mammals grieve and we humans have the ability to grieve from age two. How we grieve explains why we would want to avoid it: we cry, we scream, we feel bad, then we feel worse, and it seems that nothing will ever change. This goes on and on, back and forth with highs and lows. To grieve is to go on this bumpy ride of sadness, fear, and anger.

Once, while walking with a friend on a crowded street in Chinatown in San Francisco, I heard blood-curdling screams from a child somewhere on the crowded sidewalk. I looked for him, suspecting terrible abuse in progress. When I found him, I saw that he was crying so intensely and loudly only because his sister had taken a toy away from him. The volume of the shrieks did not seem to match the loss incurred. Suddenly, I was struck with a realization and said to my friend: "That's how we would sound if we were to cry for all that has been taken away from us!" *I have cried that way many times since.*

Grieving is our natural innate program for dealing with losses of any kind. To fear loss is to fear the feelings that arise in grief: sadness, anger, and fear itself. We fear facing the sadness that italicizes the loss, the anger that it happened, the fear that there is no replacement or ultimate comfort for us. To love is to feel all these feelings and to experience losses of many kinds. To fear grief, to refuse to open that inner program, is therefore to refuse to open ourselves, the heart of the fear of love. These feelings are also the foundations of our lively energy, which diminishes when we refuse to feel grief.

It is understandable that we fear grief. Our concept of self and our healthy development in childhood depended on the presence and love of our parents. To be bereft of the love we needed and to feel the grief of that lacuna was overwhelming. Our grief program was not yet mature enough to handle it. We felt terror, powerlessness, abandonment, and isolation. These embroideries around our feeling of grief remained in us cellularly as equations with grief. To feel grief or even to expect to feel it brings up all those archaic terrors. We fear grief now because it means becoming an orphan! The work, paradoxically, is to grieve and let go of the hurts, disappointments, and losses of childhood. Only then can we face current griefs and thereby let love in with all the sadness, anger, and fear in its train. Only those honest and brave enough to feel these uncomforting feelings can make room for the joyous feelings that spring from love when grief has passed!

Most crises are about loss and grief. You may notice, after a period of stress, crisis, or depression, that a physical fear reaction occurs. You are not afraid of anything in particular but you can feel the adrenaline pumping. That may be the fear element of the grief you just experienced. It is catching up with the sadness or anger you allowed yourself to feel. Grief wants to complete itself and does so sometimes whether we join in or not. This is the paradoxical "wisdom of no escape" referred to in Buddhism.

We were taught in public school days how important it was to be determined, to stay with it, to make sure we would win. One of the conditions of existence is not: "you will always be a winner." Sometimes, no matter how hard you try, things do not work out. "I am bound and determined to get him back, but he does not want to come back and, therefore, no matter how determined I am, it is not going to work." There comes a point when the universe steps in and declares to us, "This isn't your turn to have what you want." When that occurs, it would be good to let go of determination, because it could be a way of avoiding appropriate grief. "Stick with it and be determined" could have been invented by those who were afraid of loss and the consequent feelings of grief! What looks courageous could be a mask for a deep terror of the feeling of sadness.

Trungpa Rinpoche, the Tibetan Buddhist teacher, explains the attitude of choicelessness: instead of remaining determined, you are simply open to what the universe wants to have happen for you. He says, "Choicelessness is having no room to turn around and retrieve anything from the past. Things get very clear when you are cornered but not held captive. When you have no choice, you give up. This letting go leads to a sense of true richness and power, then true identity with your practice happens because you appreciate the teachings that created this space for you, but you do not have to make a cup to find space. Space is everywhere." To allow the space to open up and just to be in it without having to fill it with what I think I am supposed to have or be takes genuine courage. That is the courage that results from the practice of the program of change proposed in this book.

> *The heart itself cannot break, for its very nature is soft and open. What breaks open when we see things as they are is the protective shell of ego identity we have built around ourselves in order to avoid feeling pain. When the heart breaks out of this shell, we feel quite raw and vulnerable. Yet that is also the beginning of feeling real compassion for ourselves and others.*
>
> —John Welwood
> *Ordinary Magic*

FEAR AND EGO

*My destiny is to create more consciousness. The sole pur-
pose of human existence is to kindle a light in the darkness of mere being.*   —Jung

Our ego is the center of our conscious rational life and is
functional when it helps us fulfill our goals in life. It becomes
neurotic and dysfunctional when it distracts us from our
goals or sabotages them. Behind every neurosis is a fear that
has not been addressed or resolved. "Neurotic" means repetition of archaic ways of protecting ourselves against what no
longer truly threatens us. This is what Jung describes aptly as
"defeat by the unreal." Fear is therefore the foundation of the
dysfunctional behavior and the neurotic choices of our ego.

Ego is a device for believing you are separate, in control,
entitled to an exemption from the conditions of existence.
"Your choice to use this device enables it to endure," says the
Course in Miracles. The neurotic ego presents itself either with
arrogant, inflated grandiosity or with deflated, victimized
self-abasement. It is always in an extreme condition. Fear and
dualism are the moving forces behind the dysfunctional ego,
both inflated and deflated.

The Self, which Jung calls "the God archetype" within, is
the center and circumference of the entire psyche and is both
unconscious and conscious. The Self is an "objective psyche"
unlimited by individual personality (ego) yet requiring it for
full human wholeness. The Self is the same in everyone:
unconditional love, perennial wisdom, and the power to heal
ourselves and others. Our psychological work is to bring our
ego into the service of the Self, to design our every thought,
word, and deed to show the love, wisdom, and healing that
we were born with. We then articulate in our mortal lives an
immortal love, wisdom, and healing. Our spiritual work—
and destiny—is simply to be willing to allow this process and
to be receptive to the graces always available to us to fulfill it.

We know we are integrating ourselves effectively when we are on a spiritual path and, at the same time, remain functional in daily life. Our psychological work is to dismantle our neurotic ego in favor of our functional ego. The functional ego is the best vehicle for the emergence of the Self. It is the only horse that can be responsive to the gracing wind! In egocentrism, the ego acts as if it were the center of psyche rather than only the center of consciousness. This is being possessed by the archetype of Self rather than relating to it. The healthy individuated ego can endure the arrival of the Self with all its power. It welcomes its own de-thronement in favor of the true heir: the riches of love, wisdom, and healing.

St. John of the Cross says: "Swiftly, with nothing spared, I am being completely dismantled." This is the true fate of the neurotic ego. Nothing less is required for wholeness than the total dissolution of the neurotic fear-bound ego so that it can be re-constituted with no fear of the Self and then act in an axis with it. Since the Self is love, the ego actually fears love. This is the pivotal irony of our life's challenge.

Ego love is conditioned by fear of having less and desire for having more. Only unconditional love integrates us. Relationships provide the most powerful tools for the dismantling of the illusions of our controlling and entitled egos! Intimacy and love release us from the ego-bound world. A mutuality makes us whole. Love is reciprocal individuation. To let someone love us and to love someone in return is to enter the world where the ego is divested of its arrogance and its fear of losing itself in the embrace of another. Ironically, what we most fear (the loss of ego) is what most can help us toward wholeness! We have heard the phrase: love means letting go. Did we ever imagine that what has to be let go of is our own neurotic ego with its attachment to control and narcissism? "Without the conscious acknowledgment of our fellowship with those around us, there can be no synthesis of personality," says Jung.

Both Buddhism and western psychology have the same

view of functional ego. Both see the functional ego not as innate but as evolving out of our relations with others. What we call identity is an ever-reorganizing collection of internalized beliefs gathered from our past encounters with the world. But our mind fools us into seeing it as stable, unchanging, and solid. This sense of ego identity is the subject of both western and eastern psychologies. The Freudian concern was: lack of sense of self. The Buddhist concern is: how perdurance of the sense of personal, separate identity (ego) is our deepest source of suffering. "The death of the body is accompanied by much less pain than the death of the ego," says Steve Levine.

Our ego is our capacity for light; the Self is the light itself. Our destiny is to bring more and more consciousness to what is now unconscious, "to kindle a light in the darkness of mere being," as Jung says. Love and oneness are the moving forces behind the Self, which is displayed in the actions and choices of our functional ego.

But we have to be somebody before we are nobody. The issue is not self or no self but both self and no self in phase appropriate order. We do the work of forming a fully developed functional ego. Therapy is meant to get this process back on track when it becomes derailed or arrested at the identity-formation stage! The healthy ego is not the one we let go of. It is the inner representation of the ego that is the target. Spiritual awakening is not the dissolution of something real but recognition of the essential unreality that we have called our self. The Dalai Lama says: "This seemingly solid, concrete, independent, self-instituting I under its own power...actually does not exist at all."

We do not destroy the ego or the Self, only the boundary between them. The ego is the hero that struggled successfully to free itself from unconscious forces, first paradise, then perils, then Home. The ego and the Self refer to different experiential levels of one archetypal process: "This perishable nature is meant for imperishability; this mortal frame is meant for immortality," as St. Paul says. The inflated ego has feared its true inflation!

Our ego masquerades as the Self when it is driven by power motivation, rigid orthodoxy, control of others, and belief that we are entitled to special treatment, to be loved and served by everyone! These wishes are all based on fear. We might find success in manipulating the world to our own advantage. The ego gets away with its controlling ways for many years. It can even be phase appropriate to growing up. In fact, the ego has to become strong because of the danger of absorption by the Self when it is finally encountered. In addition, letting go is how we grow from dysfunctional to functional to integrating ego and Self. We have to have an ego to let go of! If our ego "fails" in the dismantling of its defenses, we remain in the state that Joseph Campbell calls "hell: being stuck in ego."

We cannot individuate unless the ego cooperates by doing what it takes to make it happen. It involves a long ride on the wind-horse of grace and effort. The self rides ego to beatific vision. "The soul does nothing if you do nothing; but it can light a fire if you chop wood; if you make a boat it becomes the ocean," writes Robert Bly in *Iron John*. What does the soul ultimately do? It reveals the divine nucleus of human psyche: the Self as the true center of personality. This leads to what the Romans called: "Amor fati," the love of one's fate. It is the ability to live with passion in any version of "what is," to say Yes unconditionally to the conditions of our human existence. The final paradox is that assent to mortal conditions is the horse that carries us to transcendence of them.

THE PAST OF FEAR: CELLULAR MEMORY

Attired with stars we shall forever sit,
Triumphing over death and chance and thee, O time.
—Milton

In our factual memory are such facts as: Albany is the capital of New York; Jefferson is the third president; summer follows spring; I attended Columbus School. These facts bring up no feeling reaction in your body. They are known, as it were, from the neck up.

The cellular memory of facts and experiences, however, connects mind and body: my body recalls that showing my true feelings in childhood led to a put-down. A slammed door meant that Dad was home and drunk. The specific fact/event may be forgotten, but the bodily reaction remains: a slam brings up terror.

Deep in our psyche, time stands still. What happened in the past is still happening now. This is what Heidegger means when he says: "The dreadful has already happened." An early loss of someone we loved, for example, created a shocking thud in our psyche. It is still reverberating. It will show up in an irrational fear that if we really love someone or something very much, we will lose that person or thing. Our experience of love has been indelibly stamped with the possibility of loss and abandonment. The irrational nature of this fear and its powerful bodily resonance are the clues to its being pre-verbal. In fact, in any panic or crisis we often revert to our worst fear and our most disabling belief. This powerlessness is another way to tell we are facing something from childhood. Our adult self would dismiss the irrationality and soon feel powerful in the face of such inappropriate fear. Our child-cellular memory has no such skills. An exercise that may help is to place your open hand over the place in your body where you feel the churning of fear and speak soothingly to your inner child. This simple mirroring of your archaic pain works exponentially in reducing its intensity.

On the other hand, if you have resolved something that happened in your childhood, then it can finally become a simple fact, and be remembered with no bodily flutter. When that happens, you know it has been totally absorbed, it has become "flat-line." There is a Zen saying, "An enlightened act leaves no wake."

The reason we stay in our head so much is because the factual memory is so safe. There is no shakedown reaction, no pain. The more you remain in your mind, the less you are in touch with your body. It is like a seesaw. You can push fear up into your mind, and turn it into a rationalization, or you can let it go farther down into your body. That is where you will have access to healing. You have to feel the fear fully in order to deal with it. You never really find out the full color scheme of your emotions if you are continually rationalizing them away.

The excretion of adrenaline, which happens when you are afraid, has, as one of its effects on the brain, the *encoding of memory*. When you were originally scared by something, you were conditioned by its fearsome stimulus and you may then remain afraid of it all of your life. Sometimes a fear from early childhood will arise because of certain present stimuli that remind you of it. Your mind may have forgotten the stimulus but the "messenger molecules" imprinted by adrenaline, always remember. They turn on and you find yourself in the fear mode. You do not know how you got there, having been involuntarily clicked into it by an unnoticed stimulus that hearkens to an unremembered time.

It is this automatic response that is the origin of our neurotic fears. Neurotic connotes repetition and unreality. We are fearing something in the present that was only dangerous in the past. We are still afraid of what is no longer really fearsome. Rollo May's words fit here: "Freedom is in the capacity to pause between stimulus and response." When we cannot *pause*, we cannot *handle* fear. Attention to our feeling is, of course, just such a healing pause.

Sometimes when everything is going well, you will notice fears come up and you do not understand why. The cellular memory could account for it. It is as if some of the unresolved fears and issues of early life wait, like courtiers, in the antechamber of our bodies for their turn to be granted an audience. The King has up till now been unwilling to hear their suit. Now the time has come and the door to the throne room has opened. During the years when you were wondering whether your spouse was having an affair, or your kids were abusing drugs, these archaic fears could not be heard. Your whole reign was taken up with other more pressing issues. When the kingdom is at peace, there is time for the pleas that have waited for decades past. *Is this why I made sure I kept the screen full?*

A specific fear looks for a general "folder" in which to place itself. You experience a loss and a grief reaction occurs. Each grief opens the entire grief historical program imprinted cellularly in you. Everything in that "program" has been opened and will have to be dealt with eventually. You are sad that someone died but you also automatically feel fear about how lonely you will be when all the kids leave. You say to yourself, "Where did this come from?" The fear came up regarding the person who died and it scanned all the fears that you were feeling or have felt and attached itself to one of them. It looked for a folder and placed itself inside. These folders are old and have primitive titles: "All is lost!" "This will never get better!" "I will fall apart!" "I am lonely and inconsolable."

An example: "They are Coming to Get Me" is not a real fear. This fear lies somewhere in the category of paranoia and irrationality. A way to handle this fear is to notice it and to say, "Oh, now I am in the 'They are Coming to Get me' folder" and then to go on with your life normally. Do not do anything to stop "them" because they are not coming after you anyway. When you do nothing to stop them, nothing to console or distract yourself, you simply let the fear sit there until it is replaced by the next stimulus. When you type nothing new into a file, it will close all by itself.

These primordial fears are what make movies work. Writers and directors look for just such folders as these because they contain instinctive, primal, archetypal fears and feelings that we all have, and they turn them on so we are impacted in a dramatic, powerful way by what we see on the screen. Drama and films are lively also because they show a character who wants something. Conflict then arises as someone/thing tries to stop him from getting it. The obstacle is the threshold guardian that tests his commitment to getting it. It all begins with knowing what one wants. The lively energy is in that knowing and in the response to the conflict around it. Fear is what stops and interrupts our lively resourcefulness.

Fear also prevents us from knowing what we want, e.g.: what do I want in this relationship? If your answer is "sex" you are probably afraid to know what you really want. It would make you too vulnerable to say: to be held, to be cared about, etc. Fear may also prevent you from entering and duking out a relationship conflict. You might choose to leave the relationship instead. Such fears cut off our lively energy even though in the doing of all these defensive things, we may look lively.

If it is true that many fears are cellular, it would stand to reason that you cannot think yourself out of a fear. You cannot say, "Well, I do not think I will be afraid of that any more now that I have understood it or been through it." Fear can activate itself automatically in every cell of your body. Your mind cannot control it. "I have learned my lesson and in my next relationship I will know enough not to be so afraid of abandonment." But it will come up in spite of any lessons you have learned because it is not a brain/mind response. It is a body/mind reaction.

You may sometimes react without even knowing that you are reacting. Your rational mind will supply many reasons for your fear of closeness or of commitment. You might not even use the word afraid: "I am uncomfortable because he is constantly pawing me. I am uncomfortable because he is with me every minute. I am uncomfortable because he wants to get married and I do not."

Another example is automatic defensiveness, a central characteristic of the ego. Someone gives you feedback and you immediately come up with an explanation that defends your position. You attempt to justify your behavior, to prove to the other person that you are right. That automatic explanation which springs out of your mouth every time someone gives you feedback or criticism, or judges you, or complains about your behavior, may be a cellular response. It is the scared ego protecting itself. Somewhere between the perceived attack and the reflex defense is not a pause but a fear: you might be shown to be wrong and therefore that you might not be loved. The final primitive fear-leap is that you will not survive. That cellular fear displays itself in the defensive remark. In addition, fear obstructs or vitiates clear thinking anyway. On the one hand, you are thinking up explanations and, on the other hand, you cannot really think clearly because the fear is getting in the way!

A friend says, "Please do not slam the door so hard when you get in my car." You might say, "In my car you have to slam it hard so I am used to doing it that way." That may come out automatically and you cannot catch yourself in time to stop it. In such a situation, you might just try *adding* something like, "I'm scared." That would be such a courageous thing to say! "I am really scared when I hear you say anything vaguely critical because that could mean that you do not like me. See how primitive I am!" To create a pause between the stimulus and your reaction, add a truth to every defensive answer. For a healthy adult, the truth is the only defense and the best resource.

THE STIFLED SCREAM

Most of our fears are encoded in our bodies because of early terrors. Experiences have stamped us with a pattern of fear and we keep feeling it cellularly without even knowing its name. Some early events in life may have been so powerful in their impact that they evoked a scream of pain or grief. If you lived in a household where feelings were not allowed or encouraged, you may have had to stifle that appropriate cry. (This silenced reaction may have become a template for later life.) You may be committed to the trick of minimizing the impact of events so that you never do scream anything out, no matter how painful.

Abandonments or neglect may have had a powerful impact but your mental appraisal of the event had to be much more subdued: "After all, my father worked hard so he could not really be present in an emotional way. My mother had so many problems of her own, she had no time for me." These statements might be ways of protecting ourselves from the full feeling-impact of the original events. The blood-curdling scream that was occurring within us in that house of absences had to be repressed. The harm was, however, compounded by the rationalization by which we told ourselves no harm was meant.

The phrase "what was meant" is totally unintelligible to the body. The body does not know anything about the intentions in the mind of another person. "Oh, yes, my mother left, but she had to leave because she was under great stress. So I do not really think of it as an abandonment. It was just necessary." The mind knows about those explanations but the body does not. All that matters cellularly is what happened. Every cell of your body felt abandoned. Perhaps you kept making adjustments to the volume control of that inner scream so that it never reached the outside. Eventually you may have lowered the volume so much that not even you could hear the screams. *We are a long way from Chinatown!*

This can be true for childhood or for adult relationships. The terrible betrayal or the rejection you felt in a relationship which now you look back at in a rational, clear-headed way might originally have been an event that made you want to scream with pain. But you had already learned that screaming was not acceptable and so it became another silent scream. This scream still wants to happen and its repression makes your body less flexible, less graceful, more tense. All those adjustments that we made to accommodate other people's needs or to make them stay with us might have been silencers of the full report of the gunfire within. In fact, you might be screaming right now and not know it. *As I write this I am aware of the deep pain that is behind each word.* There is a poem by Emily Dickinson that states this so well:

> *A great hope fell*
> *You heard no noise*
> *The ruin was within*
> *Oh cunning wreck that told no tale*
> *And let no witness in....*
> *A not admitting of the wound*
> *Until it grew so wide*
> *That all my life had entered it*
> *And there was room beside....*

The truth hurts. It is often aversively conditioning to know the truth. An event occurs and the truth of it impacts itself upon you immediately. Instead of rushing in with an explanation that excuses the other person because of his or her good intentions, you allow the full impact to hit you: "What a terrible betrayal!" That is the truth of the matter and the realization of the betrayal creates pain. Pain is an aversive conditioner. It conditions you to act in such a way that you will not feel pain again. You figure out: "All I have to do is come up with a story that explains it away: 'He really did not mean to betray me.'" I thus preserve myself from the pain. I turn the volume of the scream down and I feel much better. Actually, I have turned myself down.

Later in life, I will lie to myself over and over again having learned in this way to quiet the pain. If I let myself know the truth, it would be so painful I might not be able to stand it. The aversive conditioning comes from the truth. The reinforcement comes from the lie. We will stop telling ourselves the truth and we will stop expressing the truth of our feelings.

If the child inside, the scared child, cannot tell us about his nightmare of the past, or his nightmare of the present, how can we ever console that child? *How can I listen to my own nightmare if I have repressed my body's reaction to what happened?* When something occurs, I can attend to the impact before the intention in the mind of the other person. In childhood there was no way to do that. It was just glossed over and life went on: Time for dinner. Get ready for school. Button your jacket. There was no pause that makes the freedom to feel not only legitimate but complete.

When the other person makes an excuse about something that he or she has done to explain it away, you might say, "I want to hear what you have to say, but first I want to tell you about the impact it had on me." That would be the assertive response. First I tell you about what I feel and then you can say whatever you want about your intentions. Impact takes precedence over intention every time. If only we had followed this simple rule we would not have so many repressed voices inside us!

When we notice a connection between our present fears and their origins in early life, we are finding out how much of our identity is designed by fear. Is *fear the architect of me?*

PRESENT FEAR: REAL AND UNREAL

Macbeth said, "Present fears are less than (our) imaginings." Fear is subjective. It is often a belief in you, the subject. The object is not necessarily fearsome in reality. Fear is a subjective body/mind response to a real or *imagined* danger. Since fear is subjective, it would stand to reason that it could sometimes be appropriate, i.e., coincide with reality. I fear something that really is fearsome. You come to visit me with your dog that has a habit of biting bald-headed Italians. I fear this dog appropriately because of his history. My fear is also appropriate because I am not equipped to protect myself from a dog that bites. You come over with a Chihuahua, and I have a terrible fear that he is the carrier of TB. This is not appropriate. It is a neurotic fear of mine based on a false belief. In this instance, I have a fear that does not match reality in any way. There is no evidence nor history to support my belief. Appropriate and inappropriate are distinguished by what the record shows!

Anxiety is a subjective response to a danger that is imagined or unclear. Fear refers to a response to something that is clearly believed to be threatening. A premonition is a form of anxiety. A premonition is a foreboding or presentiment, a sense that something bad is about to happen. Premonition comes from the Latin word, *monitum*, which means warning. It is a warning from your psyche. Paranoia is the delusion that you are being persecuted or that everything that is happening refers to you. It also includes grandiosity, a belief in grand illusions about oneself.

A phobia is a persistent irrational fear that leads to a set of elaborate rituals which are meant to avoid it. This is a learned response, and may be related to something that happened in early life. It responds to behavioral methods, such as positive reinforcement, desensitization, etc. Desensitization means acting with the fear, in gradual increments of confrontations with the threat. For instance, if you have a fear of snakes, you might first become comfortable with the word snake, then with pictures of a snake, then with a video of a snake, then with going to the zoo and standing ten feet away while looking at one, etc. You can free yourself from the phobia in just such a gradual way.

It is remarkable that appropriate fear meets the danger with the skill to handle it or seeks to work on learning to handle it. I flee or fight in accord with my skills at the time. In neurotic fear, I cannot quite fight effectively and I cannot quite flee effectively. No matter what I do, the fear remains. I cannot run away from it and I cannot fight it. I do not get on with my life. In neurotic fear therefore, we are fearing our own inability to handle what we may feel or how powerless we may be. This is the essence of neurotic fear: not the fearing of the thing itself but our powerlessness in the face of it. We believe we are defenseless and resourceless. *I am pausing as I write this and asking you to pause too: these words carry such pain, don't they, and so familiar too.*

An experiment was done with rats before we had much consciousness about cruelty to animals. Two groups of rats were put into cages of different sizes. One group had very little room to move. The other group could run from one end of the cage to the other. Both groups were then scared in the same way. The ones who could not run developed heart problems. The ones that could run had hearts that remained healthy. It is not stress that hurts us but the inability to handle it, the fact—or sense— of no alternative, no escape.

WHAT IS NEUROTIC FEAR?

Neurotic fear is like a cat's dread of water:
there is really nothing to be afraid of
but he still acts as if it were seriously dangerous
and cannot get over his fear.

Neurotic fear disguises itself. It will often not even tell us its name. Knowing the identity of something is power, as the story of Rumplestiltskin illustrates. The main characteristic of neurotic fear is that it hides its real face from us. It goes by many aliases: embarrassment, reluctance, caution, secretiveness, inhibition, worry, indecision, shyness, uncomfortableness, even inability. "I cannot do it" might be a disguise for "I am afraid to do it." In recovery from an addiction, the first step is admitting who I am. I call myself by name. When I call myself by name I break through the disguise system. I articulate my truth.

A way to tell that you are hiding a fear is to look at your pastimes. You may have a fear of intimacy and of intimate conversation. Some of our activities, relationships, or hobbies may be disguises for the fear of aloneness, or lack of stimulation, or boredom. But you may never call them by that name.

I may also, in this regard, ask myself the question: "Is the pastime I choose one that provides a snack for the restless ego or is it one that provides food for the soul?" You can tell the difference between eating a doughnut or listening to Mozart. If you are feeding your soul, you are probably not being fooled by fear.

As we saw earlier, fear can be masked by rationalizations: statements that are meant to justify our actions. They are usually true statements and so we are easily fooled by them. Rationalization is another sentry, continually on duty guarding the prisoner: fear itself. His task is very simple: make sure this fear never gets out of its cell. Once you realize that the protective devices are the ones protecting the prisoner, not you, everything changes. After all, the prison guard is in prison too!

> *Here lies the body of Mike O'Dea.*
> *He died defending his right of way.*
> *His cause was just, his will was strong,*
> *But he's just as dead as if he'd been wrong.*

We have that Mike O'Dea inside, who would rather be dead than wrong. (Only the inflated ego would die really!) It is part of our work to catch ourselves in the habit of ego.

If you were to give up rationalization, you might start to know yourself as one rationalization after another. Could there be something between these rationalizations? Yes, there is. There is the space, the breath, the pause. That pause and space of calm abiding is your true self, unhindered by fear and its rationalizations.

If, pausing, you were really to look at yourself, a need that you always wanted fulfilled by your parents would be fulfilled at last. You sought an engaged loving focus from them upon you. This is called mirroring. (Such focus was their pause between the moments of their own dramas!) You would finally be giving that to yourself. That is why it is such a healing thing to know yourself. The adult is the one who found a way to give to himself, or herself, the very goods that he or she tried in vain or unsuccessfully to acquire from his or her parents. We mirror ourselves, i.e., give ourselves permission to be authentic—the opposite of defended by ego. "Defensive" is ultimately the same as scared. *I will take the pause that refreshes. Instead of rationalizing with my thoughts and words, I will simply pause and notice what I am up to. I will show my hand, admit how scared I am.*

The next characteristic of neurotic fear is the belief that things will never get better, never change. This has to be an illusory perspective since obviously nothing stays the same all the time. Things get better and get worse, arise and fall, appear, disappear, and reappear. We usually fear change and here we are fearing no change! Fear in this context is the equivalent of believing that there is no alternative. It is the opposite of lively energy, which is filled with the irrepressible discovery of more and more alternatives. In fact, joy is precisely the discovery of an alternative: "I thought it had to be this way and now I find out there is another way to do it." This gives me a sense of joy and empowerment. The essence of joy is empowerment. Victims weep; choice-makers rejoice.

Since fear takes alternatives away, it depletes you of your lively energy. When someone controls you, that person takes away your alternatives and thereby disempowers you, i.e., destroys your options: "Do it my way and no other way." A controlling person obstructs your experience of joy, power, and aliveness, if you allow it. This is why neurotic fear and being controlled damage your self-confidence. Self-confidence is the belief, the trust, that you can handle whatever comes up for you.

When you look back to your childhood, you think of all the ways adults may have tried to repress you: "Do not do this, do that." Perhaps you can truthfully say that you did those things anyway: "They couldn't stop me." It would follow that if you are stopped now, you must be the one stopping yourself, because "they" cannot stop you. Once that finally becomes clear, you realize you are the one in charge of your life, that you have a "no" still inside. In the final analysis, you are not the victim of someone who is controlling unless you choose to be. "A slave is someone who waits for someone else to set him free," says Ezra Pound.

Neurotic fear bullies us with the tyranny of what *might* happen. This fear also contains insistence that you are entitled to have things be otherwise. Such entitlement to exemption from the conditions of existence is the other major component of the neurotic ego. I desire for its excitement what I fear for its consequences. Both fear and desire bring up adrenaline, the addictive substance that may account for all of this neurotic behavior. I want to maintain the adrenaline rush of anxiety. The alternative is healthy excitement which is our lively energy! The service of Yom Kippur says: "Alas for those who do not sing, they die with their song still inside them." Lively energy is the power to feel, to let go and move on with joy. It increases to the extent that it is not burdened, cocooned over, with unresolved fears. The layers of neurotic ego form just such a cocoon in which awaits the spellbound butterfly of pure energy. This is "the dearest freshness deep-down things...." Gerard Manley Hopkins refers to.

Neurotic fear is also *obsessive,* i.e., continually occurring, unwanted thoughts, or compulsive, i.e., continually occurring, unwanted behavior. Perhaps there is a key to my fear from my compulsive behavior in demanding a perfect partner, one who will fulfill all my needs. These are the needs I missed out on in early life. I seek their fulfillment compulsively now. In other words, I seek what I cannot be satisfied with now. What I compulsively seek and do not receive in relationships is a cause for grief. If in childhood you were often neglected, not listened to, or your feelings did not matter, you may compulsively seek and easily attach yourself to someone who does pay attention to you. But this attachment really gives you information about what you missed in childhood and how you need to grieve it. Only that which is grieved and let go of can be fulfilled in adult life. The completed griefwork installs in us the capacity for fulfillment of what we lost. Ungrieved needs cannot be satisfied in any way; grieved needs can be satisfied in moderate ways. More and more in our journey through this book, we are seeing the connection between fear and the avoidance of grief.

What I compulsively seek and cannot hold signals what I need to grieve. But what I compulsively seek and do achieve, masks a *fear of its opposite.* I have a compulsive need to succeed. I am continually competing at work. This compulsion masks a fear of its opposite—the fear of failure. My compensatory behavior is repressing the fear. You may say to yourself, "What's wrong with fearing failure?" It lacks flexibility. It is human to succeed sometimes and fail at other times and we have the capacity to be able to handle both. The person who compulsively needs to achieve and to succeed is the one who cannot handle failure when it occurs. Fear is about just such self-doubt about our ability to handle what may happen.

To be fully human means to be able to dock on both banks of the river of life. Sometimes I fail—I can handle that. Sometimes I succeed and I can handle that. Succeeding does not puff me up and make me arrogant. Failure does not decimate my self-esteem and make me despondent. Success at something means that I have achieved my full potential. I have a certain potential and I activate it fully. The fear of success is the same as the fear of activating your full potential, the fear of having power. It is ultimately the most daunting fear of all, the fear of being yourself, the self that may not meet with others' standards for approval. Look at this poem by Emily Dickinson:

We never know how high we are,
Till we are asked to rise.
And then if we are true to plan
Our statures touch the skies.
The Heroism we recite
Would be a normal thing
Did not ourselves the Cubits warp
For fear to be a King.

Why would we be afraid to find out who we are? First, because to have all the power that is really mine I will have to be more responsible. Second, I have noticed in subtle ways that people think of me as strange when I am in any way unique, and I will be unique if I have all of my powers. Put those two together and it becomes unsafe to let our power become manifest.

Every neurotic fear has a history. Something must have been unsafe in childhood in order to have become a neurotic fear now. The definition of neurotic includes repetition of an old response to a now vanished stimulus. For instance, when you were left alone, without your parents present, you felt unsafe. The adrenaline of that terrifying moment encoded itself and associates aloneness with abandonment now. As we saw above, just under our ego's security is a layer of primitive fears for every occasion. Here is an example: you are standing alone, believing you have been stood up at the train station. You presume your friend does not love you anymore. A deep sense of abandonment has arisen from a minor mishap. He arrives tardily and you feel a sense of assurance that seems bigger than the occasion for it. You guess that an old terror has just visited you. What we consider our most deeply buried fears are in the shallowest of graves.

I look out my window in the polluted desert city and see the fig tree and the pomegranate tree. I know that in this environment they will never be the full-blossoming, fruit-bearing trees that they could be. They will squeeze out some fruit but it will never be as big and juicy as their species is capable of. Why? Because they are not receiving the rain they need nor the pure air they require. The universe is allowing them to have a full career on this planet without ever being fully themselves, and it will allow us the same thing. The universe will allow us to go through the rest of our life without ever being fully ourselves. The only difference is that we can water ourselves and change our air. We sometimes refuse to do this for a season or even for all four seasons, our whole life.

At the same time the universe may not let us easily get away with not being fully ourselves. The resolution of fear is part of our journey toward wholeness, a wholeness that wants to happen. Emma Jung said: "An inner wholeness presses its still unfulfilled claims upon us." Could it be that all those people and events that scare us are thereby actually working in the service of our inner wholeness, making us confront our core fears? Is this how wholeness presents its bill? Can this be the ultimate and most terrifying and most liberating synchronicity of all: everything happening to me is aimed at exposing and healing my core fears? I have attracted this person into my life to show me my hidden fears. We keep meeting the very people who make us confront our disowned selves. In our dreams we keep meeting characters who symbolize and dramatize what is unlived in our lives. The work goes on day and night, by our effort and by the grace of assisting forces.

In the ancient city of Tanagra there was a ritual feast of Hermes each year. A young man walked around the city carrying a ram on his shoulders. The people followed him in a procession, with flowers and incense. This ritual commemorated how Hermes, in the form of a shepherd, carried a ram around the city when it was beleaguered and under siege. He thereby symbolized his commitment to carry the frightened city to safety and then did so. Hermes is the messenger god, the mediator, between heaven and earth. This is an example of a healthy ritual for externalizing the experience of the fear.

The scared population, who were being attacked from out-side, and had so few defenses, saw that Hermes was carrying them on his shoulders and they trusted that this would equip them spiritually for what they were not equipped for physi-cally. The spiritual world touches the material world and the god says, "Your own limited powers require a supplement. I am your higher power and I am actually carrying you. You can trust that you will survive."

There *is* a part of this work of integrating fear that is beyond us, that can only be done by the good shepherd who walks around our world with us, who has power that we do not have. As stated before, not all of the work is done by our ego. There is another force that comes into play. It is a force that has the power to bring things back to life when every-thing seems done for. It is known variously as the grace of God, a Higher Power, the Self, the universe, Spirit.

STORY AND SILENCE

We have often heard the expression: the silence within. What is this silence? It is our human nature when it coincides with universal nature. Our man-made dramas then become peripheral: ground not figure. A silence—full of sanity and serenity—opens up as our natural (spiritual) self comes into focus. I joyfully discover that I am more than my story. It is my ego that has a story; my soul is a silence.

The ego's neurotic threads: fear, desire, judgment, shame, blame, expectation, and attachment to outcome, are all part of the tapestry that the ego weaves to distract us—and entertain us! To find myself is to land in the silence of what is as it is, beyond the dramas of ego. This is what is meant by being centered: not to have no story but no longer to be overwhelmed by it. I become a silent and fair witness of my life. I see more headlines and news items with fewer edi-torials!

To Do: The Old Story

Try this exercise: take an old story that you keep telling. Perhaps you have used it to garner sympathy for yourself as a victim, or to incite animosity toward someone else, or to shed some of your own distress onto others. You may thereby be stuck in your drama. To access your soul silence follow these four steps:

Feel these three feelings that lurk somewhere in your story: sadness, anger, and fear. For instance, if before you only felt angry, now let yourself feel the fear and sadness that are also surely inside you.

Accept the fact of what happened matter-of-factly!

Allow yourself to feel compassion for all the characters in your story, including yourself.

Look for the spiritual connection between your story and your destiny: How has this helped me come closer to who I was really meant to become?

After completing these steps, notice if the story has changed in these ways:

It no longer sounds quite the same as you tell it.

It is no longer necessary to tell it.

It has humor!

If the above three elements are present, you have resolved something and moved on. (If it has not worked, try again!)

Mindfulness is not meant to lead to quietism. It activates us: "The person of joy is beyond what is done and what is not done. I have no work to do in all the worlds. I have nothing to obtain, because I have all. And yet I work. In the bonds of work I am free, because in them I am free of desire...When I go beyond desire...the world of sound and sense is gone. I am free from the thought: this is mine." (Gita)

I am faced with a life-long work of integrating unconscious features of myself (both personal and archetypal) into consciousness. I become heroic in my journey through pain. An ego enriched in this way is no longer scared and held in, i.e., ego centric but is ex-centric. Wallace Stevens says: "It was when the trees were leafless, first in November, and their blackness became apparent, that we first knew the eccentric to be the base of design."

No longer conditioned by fear and desire (ego centric), I now am living in unison with and at the service of my higher self (eccentrically). This means that I have de-throned my ego. Creative consciousness is continually moving. When we interrupt the flow by over-identifying with one or another figure of the mind we are attached, stuck. Creativity stops dead in its tracks. No combination of opposites can occur and we are polarized. This is the origin of neurosis: an inner split. When it is projected on a world scale, war results.

APPROPRIATE FEAR

Neurotic defenses inhibit you and ultimately make you fear again. The neurotic defenses are: obsession, compulsion, rationalization, denial. When you engage in these, you deny your feelings and you avoid or over-react to a threat. The healthy defenses are the ones that free you and equip you to deal effectively with whatever may come up. Neurotic defenses inhibit you; healthy ones free you. An example of a healthy defense is maintaining your boundaries. Saying "ouch," or "stop," or "you cannot do that to me"—these are also healthy defenses. The unhealthy defense is: "I will go along with abuse without complaint," or, "It is not really happening," or "I will get her for this."

We have seen that in an appropriate fear, you will always notice an alternative. No exit means disempowerment. No exit means not seeing the whole picture. An alternative in healthy fear is to stand up and fight. I do not have to take this lying down. It could also be to stand your ground, not to give your territory away. Instead of staying on the road of fear, you find the side road and with it a sense of joy, the joy of finding an alternative. You do not have to be in pain. You do not have to be afraid. You can find another way.

In healthy, appropriate fear, the fear warns you. But it can do even more than that: picture yourself as the mayor of a small town, asleep late one night. The town crier comes to your door and says, "Come down to the beach right away! There's a fleet of enemy ships coming in and we have to figure out what to do about it. Maybe we'll have to warn everybody and take some action." If you are in a deep sleep then the town crier has to cry louder but if you are able to wake up easily, you hear what he says. He is the messenger or the herald who is telling you that something dangerous is happening. If you believe him, you let him lead you to the beach, and you see, out there on the dark horizon, the ships with their black flags, coming to attack. The crier has shown you exactly where the danger is. Now you make a plan to gather the other townspeople together, and plan nonviolent forms of resistance. The job of the town crier is done. He just becomes an ordinary citizen, and one of your allies.

Apply this analogy to feeling a fear. The fear is the town crier announcing to you—and it will have to be a stronger (louder) fear if you are deeply asleep, i.e., unconscious, not open, disbelieving, or very good at rationalizing! Appropriate fear is first a herald, a messenger. Secondly, it is a guide that shows you exactly where the threat is. And thirdly, it becomes an ally. Healthy people heed the crier. The neurotic way is: denying that there is any town crier, denying that he is saying anything, not going out to explore, just staying where you are, asleep, until the enemy overruns the town and you.

HOLDING ON TO FEAR?

The armor I use to protect myself actually prevents me from having full access to my powers.

Neurotic fear is sometimes used to protect the ego from the possibility of ever finding out it has a twin named ego-lessness. Egolessness happens when we fall into the gap, the space between the chapters of our experience. For instance, you can go from one relationship immediately into another because you fear that the space between might be painful, i.e., lonely. Yet true identity is precisely in the gap where we confront our fears and fearlessness begins.

We really *are* that gap or space. This is why it is so deeply trustworthy. The ego itself is a combination of fear and desire. Egolessness is freedom from the grip of fear and desire. You can never be free from fear and desire totally, not until you have reached enlightenment or sanctity. But you can be free of the grip of them. That is the egoless state. *A gap between our thoughts might be a space where our identity would reveal itself as spaciousness.* Instead, to make sure that does not happen, we attach one thought to the next. Throughout the day we create a tinny parade of one thought after another with no space.

If a space were to open up between the thoughts—a meditative space—you might feel afraid. You might feel as if you were nobody, because your identity has always been equated with your thoughts. "I'm the one who's thinking these thoughts. I think, therefore I am!" Thinking itself staves off the moment of no thought—the gap between the thoughts—the egoless state where I am my spiritual self, instead of my ego.

"The certainty that nothing can happen to us that does not in our innermost being belong to us is the foundation of fearlessness," Govinda says. The foundation of fearlessness is in the realization that this fear is all part of me, a confrontation with which is what it takes for me to be who I am. These are the experiences that had to happen in order for me to achieve my destiny. When I see this, I make an agreement with the universe instead of picking an argument with it. If fears come my way, I work with them, I deal with them, because they are part of me. And they would only be coming my way if this were the manner in which my destiny could be achieved. That is the spiritual foundation of fearlessness: how fears work to show me my honeysuckle-thistle path.

In this paradigm, you are not the object of an experience but the experience itself. You do not have to be caught in the experience of fear, you can experience it and then rest in the space beside it. We attend to our irrational fears and learn to handle them. But then we also move on to their metaphorical significance. The paradox is that the unconscious speaks to us precisely through the irrational, e.g., obsessive thoughts, compulsive behaviors, addictions. The inner self does not usually communicate through the left-brain rational mind! A fear of our house being robbed can mean fear of our self being forcibly entered. The metaphorical speaks more poignantly than the literal.

We may look back at all the years of unconsciousness or addiction and think: what a loss! We feel regret but there is still the issue of how the inner Self was using that time as a necessary *incubation* period for the new challenges that would be coming. Through the metaphor, we have reframed sleep to rest! Recovery is the bridge between these two: "It takes what it takes to get here." Even the pain was a part of the healing. *Perhaps it was less that time was wasted as that it was gathered.* There was continuity in it all. There is continuity in my life!

Could it be that something unknown to us is doing creative work in us? Unknown is unconscious. It remains unconscious precisely so that it not be contaminated by the conscious thinking mind. Every time we go beyond our habitual, conscious mind sets, we free ourselves. To let in a little chaos may be a way to access a far more imaginative set of powers! This is why the work is to accept our fear and feel it.

When you act because of fear, a cognitive deficit can occur. You start making errors in judgment and losing your intuition. You lose your perspective and the confidence to face your own reality. You become paranoid about the power of others over you or about your lack of power over yourself. Even mountain climbers that are very adept, at high altitudes where there is less oxygen, notice a deficit in their judgment. Because of this confusion, many fall, even though they are highly skilled. The same thing happens to us in the fear state.

Here are examples of trains of thought led by fear:

Regarding a risk or challenge: change means loss and if I lose I will have to grieve and if I grieve I am going to feel absolutely terrible and therefore I must not let anything change.

Regarding self-disclosure: if people really saw me as I am, they would not like me. So I hide my real self; I do not let anybody see the real me.

Regarding loneliness: if I'm alone, I will be lonely, I will feel very sad and devastated so I frantically fill my time with constant contact with other people.

Regarding intimacy: intimacy leads to abandonment or engulfment or failure or betrayal. I stay away from it.

The scared child, the prisoner inside, is creating a deficit in your thoughts and in your belief in your ability to handle things. He is marking up the walls of your mind with graffiti: "Change means loss. Self-disclosure means rejection. Aloneness means death. Intimacy means abandonment. You cannot handle anything skillfully. Stay in your cell." We build inner resources when we *accept defenselessly and take action resourcefully.*

As we saw above, most of us have had very few models for handling fear since adults usually hid their fears from us, or sometimes even took them out on us in the form of anger. If a boy believes that only cowards feel fear, there is no support for admitting or showing that he is afraid. If showing it and admitting it is the first step toward recovery, what chance does he have to grow up with honest feeling?

In addition, we all face the taboos of society which controls us by fear. Without fear, we might explore the farther regions of our identity and discover a whole new psychic territory in which we could live and lord. If I ever do notice other powers than the ones they said I had, I would find myself alone. Whatever taboos you buy into are also limitations of your identity. Identity grows to the extent to which you have explored the uncharted spaces. True identity is in the space between the injunctions.

Our destiny is an ever-increasing spaciousness and consciousness, a space that we create, somewhere between all those messages and injunctions hurled at us from the beginning of our life and even now. We suddenly find revealed a whole new way of living, a whole new way of seeing, a whole new way of feeling, a whole new way of expressing, a whole new way of composing music, or of writing poetry. Beethoven saw that Mozart had achieved the ultimate in the then current forms of musical expression. There was nowhere to go. The only thing he could do was open up a whole new space and that is exactly what he did. Where was that newly created art? It was in the space between the rules and the respected forms. Lingering there, he set himself and music free.

As we commit ourselves to keep increasing the space, our capacity to expand becomes obvious. We discover our own infinity, a microcosmic mirror of the universe. (In fact the universe is continually granting us the mirroring we may have missed in childhood!) Isis, speaking to the Pharaoh, says, "I will give you the life span of the sky." I will give you an identity as expansive as that of the universe—not an identity as limited as family traditions or curses, or society's permissions and prohibitions. How many of us could accept that gift-challenge? We might run from that to the field of right and wrong. With everything before us, we shrink back. That is a sad enigma about us.

When you see the falcon flying high above, you realize he is living out his full potential. He is doing the most he can do, stretching his wings all the way and gliding along the high air while scanning the earth below. He has no choice. But we have free will. We can choose not to expose our full potential, not ever to fly so high, not ever to sing so loud, not ever to bear all our fruit, not ever to free ourselves from all the do's and do nots, the should's and should nots. Instead we become so heavy with should's and do's that there is no room for the space, not around us, not inside us, not underneath us, not above us. When a fear comes to challenge us, it feels like a heavy impenetrable mass that cannot be dissolved. That may be happening because we are not used to seeing spaces in ourselves. We are used to staying so solid that everything that occurs seems solid too. *Could we lighten up, space out, and let the light and air through?*

Spaces will never happen to those who have chosen to live totally within the limits set by the taboos. Nor will there be space for those who impose those same limits on other people by continually controlling. As long as we are filled in, the spiritual definition of the Self, which is pure space, cannot get through to us. This is the space that is in a hollow bamboo, so that Krishna can play his song.

Our ego fears the opening of this tremendous abyss, or void, where "I will not be anybody." That is the irony. Here you are fearing being nobody when this way of being nobody is your identity: the space, the pause. Before I try to avoid fear by controlling someone, I pause and then I do not do it. That brings space in. I do not think I will control or rationalize this time; I think I will sit this one out. Then space opens, i.e., I open. Enlightened means spaced to make room for light. You do this by waking up to the criers: your feelings. Thereby you create a space for the destiny that has come your way. Since we are infinite space, there is space in us for everything to pass through. It is the Isis space that is sky. The falcon flies through, and leaves the space intact. That is the space inside us. Our identity is an inner sky, "on earth as it is in heaven." Like a cathedral, we do not take up space; we create space.

To Do: Exaggerating

A humorous way to work on primitive/neurotic fear is to exaggerate it in your mind deliberately until you find yourself laughing. For example, you fear that if you tarry to tie your shoe on your way out of the house with a friend, he may not wait for you. (This probably has a connection to some such actual event in your childhood.) You say to yourself, or, even better, aloud to him: "I fear you won't wait for me so I can't tie my shoe. I would rather trip and fall than take the chance you won't wait for me. You see, if you leave without me that will mean you don't like me, and if you don't like me, I may die." (Seeing dying as the bottom line is a good way to achieve exaggeration.) His look of perplexity will strike you funny or his laughter will get you to laugh too. Charlie Chaplin said the secret of his humor was that he played with pain. In that non-ridiculing style of humor, fear lifts away because the human brain cannot experience humor and fear at the same time.

Your parents may have only showed tenderness and warmth toward you when you were afraid. You thereby received the message: "If you want to get the goods you have to feel bad." This imprints a fear in your body because you reinforce fear with desirability. "I will get something good from the other person. He will take pity on me, show compassion toward me, hold me, be with me because I am afraid." Look back to childhood and ask: "When did my parents show the most warmth and affection?" If they showed it in the context of fear, you may have made a cellular connection in yourself between fear and love.

Once I fully resolve something, I have broken the connection of panic in the cells of my body. I have finally healed myself in the healthy way by dealing with whatever happened. To address, process, and resolve old issues, especially in the context of therapy, makes it possible to leave the past behind and move into the clean-slated present.

Look for the ways and contexts in which you feel fear and make journal entries on how they link up with childhood events or messages.

Florence

Gabriel and his son Joe left Connecticut and lived in Florence for six months. Joe then went to Pamplona to run with the bulls and travel in Spain alone. Father and son planned to meet in a month in Rome to return home to America together. Though Joe had promised to write or call, he never did, creating anxiety in Gabe. One Friday afternoon, Gabe found a card in his mail-box: "You have a telegram and were not here to receive it. We are closed for the weekend. Please come on Monday to claim it."

Gabe's first thought was that Joe was hurt or dead. He was seized with panic and then fell into a deep depression. Gabe loved his son more than anything in the world and the loss of him was intolerable. Gabe could not sleep or eat for the whole weekend. He imagined the worst. He regretted coming to Italy for this sabbatical. He lamented Joe's going off on his own. He suffered the tortures of the damned, obsessing about Joe's fate.

On Sunday, Gabe decided to walk up to Piazzale Michelangelo, where there was a panoramic view of the city and the beautiful old church of San Miniato. He walked like a robot and, with every step, felt more despondent. He even contemplated suicide. He was isolated in an impenetrable void.

Arriving at San Miniato, Gabe joined the Mass in progress without his usual enthusiasm or comfort. When the Mass ended, he walked across the grass to the panoramic viewing area. Suddenly, a voice of unknown origin spoke within him: "No matter what this telegram is about, you will be able to handle it, as you have everything else in life!" Gabe stopped in his tracks: who said that? And yes it was true! Suddenly the powerlessness gave way to a strength that surfaced from deep within him, where it had always lain but now was awakening.

He ate a pizza; he slept the night through. He went on Monday to the telegram office and read: "Your flight time for Los Angeles has been moved from 2:00 PM to 2:05 PM."

2.

How Fears Display

PANIC ATTACKS

Panic happens when we believe ourselves to be powerless. Powerlessness means: I cannot do what my body is arming me to do by the appropriate excretion of adrenaline: flee or fight. We are confronting a danger which seems unavoidable and we feel powerless in the face of it. Physically, the brain sends nerve signals to the adrenal glands. This triggers the release of adrenaline (fear) and noradrenaline (anger). There are four molecules of adrenaline for every one of anger! Noradrenaline keeps us alert and helps us concentrate. Adrenaline helps us get ready to fight or flee. It does this through the following automatic concomitant physical means:

Saliva and mucous dramatically dry up so more air can reach the lungs.

Sweat cools the body.

More blood goes to the brain as blood pressure rises.

White blood cells fight infection more efficiently.

The rate of respiration increases.

Pupils dilate to be able to see better.

Digestion is diminished.

More sugar enters the bloodstream since the liver is receiving a signal from the adrenal glands that danger is nearby.

Recovery from a burst of adrenaline takes about ten minutes. To repress fear and anger means subverting a complex bodily scenario that wants to happen. Repression attenuates the reaction and the recovery so that adrenaline remains in your system and becomes toxic. Long bouts of adrenaline lower the body's immune response.

The above description applies to fear in general and to panic attacks. You might go through stages of stress such as alarm, resistance, and then recovery. Panic attacks can also be associated with physical problems: heart disease, depression, hypoglycemia or diabetes. For instance, if you wake up feeling panic, that might be a sign of hypoglycemia since blood sugar is low in the morning. If your panic attack happens at the same time every day, it might be associated with eating or fasting and thus be related to sugar metabolism.

Panic attacks are usually short, and what devastates us is the psychological intimidation and sense of powerlessness that comes with them. The sense that you are losing control, that you are going crazy, that everything is falling apart, and you are being threatened beyond your limits, are all normal reactions during these attacks.

In a panic attack, you do not know what you are afraid of. But your mind will engage in its habit of scanning all the possibilities and attach itself to some explanation. The mind wants to fill in the gaps to avoid the sense of powerlessness. But in a true panic attack none of this works. It is an automatic physical response, probably containing any number of silent screams that are waiting to be released.

In the experience of fear and panic you meet the scared child inside. In working through fear and panic, you acknowledge an adult inside, equipped to handle these painful moments. If your family or religious training had to do only with molding the scared child and not with equipping the responsible adult, then you will never feel able to handle feelings. You remain a scared child always dependent on others to fix you. It is a stimulating challenge to find and free the adult side of your family and past. How comforting it might have been to have felt assured that we had a legitimate place in the universe no matter what! You have to ask yourself if your past gave you that kind of assurance. If it did, it was healthy; if it did not, then it is something from which to recover.

When you attune yourself to the scared child inside, the adult response comes up automatically. You will notice a sense of comfort and a sudden recognition of the adult alternative. I do not have to be stuck. I do not have to be ashamed. That sense of an alternative, a shift to adult power, is what tells you that you have succeeded in finding healing.

Juliet asked Romeo how he was able to enter her garden: "The orchard walls are high and hard to climb and the place death considering who thou art." Remember he answered: "With love's light wings did I o'er-perch these walls. For stony limits cannot hold love out and what love can do that dares love attempt." Love is daring over and over again to act with fear. When you love yourself and when you love the other you are willing to take that chance. When you act with daring over and over again you gradually change the molecular message that was encoded by all those bursts of adrenaline throughout your life.

To Do: In Case of Panic

When a panic attack happens, allow it, stay with it. Remember that panic leads to self-doubt about your body's natural way of monitoring itself. You will feel more out-of-control than you ordinarily do. It is helpful to use the paradoxical approach which is simply to act *with* the fear. Feel the fear and panic with unconditional consent, and take no action against it. This might be a way of de-fanging the panic before it overwhelms you. You cannot stop panic itself but you can stop it from taking control. Being stopped by the panic is the danger, not the panic itself.

This method of working with panic attacks continues with two more recommendations. One is to focus on a tranquil image internally. (It is useful to have some image prepared in your mind beforehand.) This can be a scene, picture, image, religious icon, etc., that you summon up and that brings serenity. Preferably, it is the image that has a history of being pleasing to you. Just the bringing of images into your mind decreases the consumption of oxygen, slows down your breathing, decreases your heart rate, lowers your blood pressure, reduces tension, and brings more blood to your brain. In other words, it reverses the components of the panic attack. Or as Emily Dickinson says, "To shut our eyes is travel." Just by shutting your eyes and focusing on the image you travel away from panic and powerlessness. Everything calms down. This is the power of an image and perhaps explains why religious images are enshrined and mediate healing.

The final feature of the handling of panic is breathing. In a panic attack, you are hyperventilating. Remember that in stress you shift your breathing from the lower part of your lungs where the diaphragmatic, deep breathing happens, to the upper part: thoracic, where shallow, quick breathing occurs. With deeper breathing from the diaphragm, you breathe into the lower lung area and that breathing reverses the panic breathing. The thoracic breath is necessary for an immediate response to fear, but here we have no object of fear, so it is not really useful. The diaphragmatic breathing is necessary for repose. You might do this with your eyes closed and counting from ten to one on each exhale. You might affirm that you are inhaling support from the universe and exhaling the panic and pressures that are weighing upon you.

This combination of the allowing of the fear, forming an image, and breathing diaphragmatically, reduces the panic dramatically.

Marvin's Miracle

Marvin is forty-two and for the past six years he has suffered from severe panic attacks. In fact, Marvin feels anxious all the time. He has the sense that butterflies are swirling in his stomach throughout the day and that every once in a while, at least weekly, he is being attacked by a pterodactyl called "paralyzing panic." The panic comes with no warning and can last from a few minutes to an hour. There is no real threat, danger, or impending disaster in Marvin's life. In fact, to the outside world, it seems that he is quite trouble-free.

He works as a physician at the local hospital, is well-to-do, drives a Mercedes, and has a large investment portfolio with secure retirement plans. He owns his own home, and has a vacation home in the mountains. Marvin has explored all the physical possibilities that can account for his fears, employing every test and technique, but nothing has helped.

Marvin's anxiety showed itself as a constant flow of adrenaline and nervousness. The panic laid him low almost entirely. He would break out into a cold sweat, not be able to talk or walk properly, lose his appetite, shake, and even occasionally collapse altogether. This could happen at any time and if he was with a patient, he had to leave immediately and often not return, while his nurse made excuses. This was exacerbated by Marvin's compulsive cleanliness and neatness. Even the slightest stain on his clothes led him to change immediately into one of the many extra garments he kept in the closet in his office. His life had become totally dysfunctional.

One day Marvin was alone in the midst of a panic attack at a park near his office. He was absently watching some young children playing in the mud with no concern at all for the state of their clothes. They were throwing mud-patties at one another with great abandon and smearing it on their faces and bodies too. They were completely oblivious to the mess they were making. Something snapped in Marvin's highly intellectual and scientific mind and he suddenly saw this pandemonium as directly applicable to his condition.

He began breathing more deeply and said over and over: "I allow this fear to trudge through me in its own muddy way and I still remain: behind it and in it and after it." This affirmation came to him the first time he allowed the panic and the anxiety with no attempt to interrupt it with anything except breathing! Soon he was breathing more openly and actually felt less anxious.

Now his panic attacks are almost completely gone and his medical colleagues are quite surprised and delighted with his progress. Marvin eats well, sleeps well, can see patients safely, and his self-esteem has risen. He thanks the children for the mud bath they gave to his psyche and he still does not understand how any of this works.

THE FEAR OF COMINGS AND GOINGS

Agoraphobia is the fear of going too far away from your personal environment. People who have this phobia may not be able to go out into a crowd without feeling panic. There is also a psychological agoraphobia which is part of the fear of abandonment. A condition of existence is that people come and go in the course of our life, yet you may feel forsaken as they go or afraid as they arrive.

The Greeks, at every crossroads, placed a symbolic statue of Hermes, the god of comings and goings, the messenger and mediator between gods and men. The Romans had special gods for the doorway; special gods for the lintel; special gods for the gate outside the house. Coming and going was associated with such fear and stress that it had to be protected by divinities. This gives us information about how ancient in our psyche is this fear.

In childhood we fear losing approval if we go, and losing our security if our parents go. In some families, you are looked upon as a traitor if you move far away once you are an adult. I may fear losing approval if I go. I may fear not being approved when I arrive at the new place. I may fear that no one will be here when I come back.

In childhood, other people decided our comings and goings. We were just moved or they moved out and left us. Comings and goings were thereby associated with powerlessness. Comings and goings were associated with scary abandonments, making it very understandable that this would be an anxiety-producing part of life ever after.

To become an adult, you have to take leave of the safe nest your parents provide, and become an individual rather than a replica of them. Their opinion can no longer be authoritative over your choices. These are our two adult tasks: to go and to be. The first task of maturity is to go, with all the challenge, fear, danger, and difficulty that may entail. Then we have to take a stand whether or not we are approved for it. The need for approval is paradoxically cut from the same cloth as the fear of individuating.

Approval means meeting with the projection of me in the other person's mind. He approves of me because I meet the standard that he carries in his head. That is the opposite of individuating in which the projections of others do not matter since I have chosen to be myself. As a separate, individuated self, I form adult-adult relationships. I form a parental bond with anyone from whom I am trying to gain or maintain approval.

The reason approval became so important is that we needed it to survive. The reason abandonment is so terrifying is that it deprives us of mirroring the fulfillment of our emotional needs that equip us to be able to relate emotionally to others. We know by unconscious instinct that approval, love, and presence by our parents or partners is necessary for our healthy development. We fear appropriately the loss or endangerment of goods so necessary to our evolution.

FOUR PARTS OF COMING AND GOING

What happens to scare you in your own adult comings and goings? Look at the four elements: First, you go out, leaving the familiar behind. Second, you are on the journey, in the process of going, facing the unknown. Third, you arrive somewhere. Fourth, you settle into a new place.

These are all areas of distress, each of which would require its own god, from the Roman perspective! You first step over the threshold, then you are en route to the next threshold; then you are crossing the new threshold.

In marriage or living together, I crossed my own threshold to come to yours. Look what I have done. I have faced the fear of going, I have crossed the threshold from the familiar where I know it is safe, and I have made the journey to a new place where it may not be safe. Do I now ask you to be a new parent or to be another adult? Do I blame you if you disappoint me?

STEPPING OUT

Leaving home means separating and letting go. It means abandoning what is familiar, taking a risk, possibly even winding up in a state of isolation. Why is it scary to go? You are confronting the fear of standing out there alone. This is the fear of just being yourself without all the things and people and habits that kept you secure. *I am choosing to be unprotected by my usual supports.* That risk is in the very action of going.

Secondly, I am leaving behind something about my identity, because here I am known as a certain person and there I will not be known as anybody and will have to establish my identity again. I will be nobody. Here my tricks and my charms work because I have polished them up and I have trained people to respond to them. There I do not know if my tricks will work. *I am starting to see that my charms and poses were ways of avoiding the fear of presenting myself just as I am. Is this all a self-disclosure issue?*

Thirdly, I will no longer be the one in charge. I will lose my sense of control; I will be at the mercy of strangers. Since I was also holding on to the sense of control, fear will flood in when I let go of it.

EN ROUTE

While I am on the journey itself, I am in a gap between where I was and where I am heading. This traveler becomes no one special. I am just one of a hundred people on a train or plane and nobody knows me here. No special treatment or attention will be shown to me. My identity and my roles make no difference. I am unprotected by any support system.

As you go, you may experience sad feelings about all the people you have left behind. The fear of going is associated with grief, regret, or guilt. You may feel sentimental or nostalgic about things or people. This is a form of light grief. All these reactions are signs of the distress, i.e., fear associated with change. You might be worried about whether you will measure up and find approval when you arrive. You might fear that while you are away, something terrible will happen at home and you will not be there to deal with it. Somebody might die and there will be no way of reaching you.

Most people easily meet other people and become open with them while traveling. For instance, you might talk about your whole life while sitting on a plane or train with a stranger. You are more open than usual. This may be an attempt to diffuse your nervous energy, anxiety, neediness, isolation, and vulnerability. It may also be an attempt to establish an instant surrogate support system! These are all forms of the fear that happens within this gap between one place and another. These fears are not based on information but on primitive dread, the panic about going.

Another way to work with these fears? You could cry at each step of the way because each step has something to do with grief. "I feel sad as I shut the door and leave my house. I think I'll sit here and cry before I go." We are not used to showing grief so appropriately and uninhibitedly.

ARRIVING AND SETTLING IN

You can determine your distress level surrounding arriving by asking yourself, "Do I demand that other people make a fuss over me?" I am visiting my friends in another state, for Christmas. Do I arrive there needy and want to see that they have made extensive preparations for my coming? Do I arrive with gifts for everyone, to be sure that they like me? Do I arrive with many compliments about their house and themselves? Do I arrive with anger—nothing here is to my liking? Do I arrive late? Do I arrive without bringing what I needed so I will have to depend on other people to take care of me? Deciding to go home earlier than planned is another sign of the general agoraphobia we may all experience to some extent. These may all be indicators of something phobic about your arrival style.

When you are settling in, do you have a strong need for something familiar around you? Do you have the need to contact home, confirming it is still there, that you are still loved there—and that no one has died! This is actually quite understandable. My identity is not portable. I am only myself when I am with my own things and my own job and my own people. This is why Ulysses was so bereft in his long travels home where, and only where, his full identity awaited him.

Yet, as I become more adult, I am myself everywhere. I am not seeking the Promised Land outside. It is not in any one place. It is an inner sense of security anywhere I am. Remember the story of St. Francis of Assisi when he decided to become a monk and his father said no. Francis took off all his clothes and said, "Now I have returned everything that belongs to you and I am starting my life over again without ties or possessions." He divested himself of everything in order to feel more himself.

Jung says, "In the intensity of the disturbance lies the value and the energy to remedy it." Our lively energy has within it all the programs (capacities) needed to face each of the stresses of life. It is not within the scope of this book to deal with pathological agoraphobia. The program for the mild agoraphobia described above is: admitting fear, feeling it, and acting as if it were not an obstacle. This is the program that we will have to work in order to release our own self-restorative energy. Power is in being the cause of the effect that you want. I want the effect of moving through it, so I stay with the cause of it all the way to the effect. We keep noticing how paradox is the style of human healing.

THE FEAR OF LETTING GO OF CRUTCHES

Movement invites attention, asks us to practice devotion to ourselves, not in a self-centered way, but as an act of loyalty. Instead of abandoning ourselves, we can learn to inhabit ourselves. The body is tremendously homesick for us, and it waits patiently for our return. Though we have ignored its invitations for years and years, when we do say yes, now, it bounds forward with great exuberance and know-how. We find that we need no training in being fully alive, that we only lacked the determination to feel our aliveness. And here it is.

—John Welwood, *Ordinary Magic*

Most of us have a fear of getting through crises—or sometimes even the day—as truly sober adults. We cannot imagine facing boredom or stress or problems without the use of caffeine, alcohol, nicotine, sugar, overeating, or drugs.

Even while not being addicts, we may be using these substances as crutches.

The body has capacities such as walking, moving, dancing, etc. The mind has the capacity to engage in logical thinking, discursive reasoning, imagination. We begin transforming these capacities to skills in early life. If, by age two, instead of being taught to walk, you were taught how to use a wheelchair and told you could not walk, then your ability to walk would atrophy even though you really had that capacity. If all your life somebody else thought for you, you would never learn how to think for yourself and that capacity would also atrophy.

If, every time your body/mind is ready to use one of its capacities, you substitute a substance that does it for you, you take a chance of having your body/mind capacities atrophy. What are these body/mind capacities? They are: to unwind, to gear up or wake up, to focus on something, to stay with a task, to take an interest in something and to be engaged in it, to feel our feelings from beginning to end: to feel the onset of a feeling and its crest, and to express it and let go of it, to grieve losses, to face fears.

We even have the capacity to get over depressing moods. ("I simply remember my favorite things and then I don't feel so bad!") We have the capacity to come down from a manic mood. We have the capacity to relax, to take a break, to jump into something, to let go. These are automatic instincts of our body/mind, endowments of our lively energy. In the course of life, we gradually learn how to access these and use them with ease. Here is an example: in order to fall asleep, we do not have to suck on a pacifier, or a bottle of warm milk. But remember that, originally, that is what it took to fall asleep. Then one day, the bottle was taken away. You screamed in protest and eventually tired yourself out and fell asleep. The next night you did the same but you realized more clearly that the theatrics did not work. You went through your withdrawal period and then you started to fall asleep naturally. No one explained how to do it; you accessed the power inside yourself that knows automatically how to put yourself to sleep, a power you still have.

But this instinct does not kick in anymore if, over and over again, instead of accessing the power within yourself, you do it with a glass of wine or a pill. The power to unwind or go to sleep gradually is replaced by the inclination to take a pill or have a drink.

In Victorian times, women fainted often. Victoria cannot handle what is going on so she passes out. While whatever is going on continues to go on and finishes itself, she is unconscious. When the whole thing is cleared up, she awakens and has nothing to face. Men did the same thing by dueling (and do it still by war). There have always been ways of avoiding the process of addressing and resolving things.

What do these surrogate capacities do? First they cover the feelings you might have in response to what is coming up in your life: I am feeling a little nervous. I do not want to feel the full feeling so I will have a drink. The alcohol somehow changes what is going on. Secondly, surrogates, such as caffeine, alcohol, marijuana, etc., replace, blockade, and ultimately extinguish our lively energy. You become split off from all the wonderful powers inside—the powers that are your lively energy.

If you have to have coffee to wake up and you need it throughout the day to get through those dull periods, perhaps it is time to ask yourself, "Am I taking the chance of killing off natural lively energies and powers that I have inside?" If every time you have to face something you turn to a substance, how can you ever learn to face anything? My adult capacity for a lively response does not arise anymore because what comes into my mind instead is an image—the image of a cigarette, the image of a cup of coffee, the image of chocolate.

We have turned our wills and our lively energies over to the care of these substances. (If every time you believe you need a drink you call someone and talk, eventually the need to drink will become the need to talk.)

Obviously this refers also to excessive TV or internet, shopping, sex, gambling, drugs, etc. The task of adulthood is to open up all the wonderful powers inside, powers waiting to be found and activated. Here is a metaphor: your new VCR comes with a manual that tells how to access all the features it has. If all you do is play tapes and nothing more because you are afraid of how complicated the other procedures are, then you never activate its full complement of powers. When you run to coffee, alcohol, etc. you are saying the same thing: "It's too hard to do it with the full use of the built-in powers."

Most of this is no longer in the realm of choice but automatic. We are having cups of coffee throughout the day, smoking cigarettes, or having some wine at the end of the day, without asking, "What is this taking the place of?" Long, habitual resort to substances, though appearing normal and innocent, shuts down our adult powers. What powers? The power to feel; the power to unwind; the power to get through things; the power to face things. *Is alcohol or sex what I have been doing with my feelings?*

The serpent of ego offers us an apple, our favorite substance, when we actually have access to a whole orchard of much more exciting fruits. Do we imagine that an apple is tastier than cherries, peaches, or pomegranates? The substances we get hung up on are flat compared to the variegated powers inside. Yet we choose the limited apple over the tasty peach out of habit or lack of imagination.

In childhood or in adulthood, significant others in our lives may have initiated us into the use of these substances. Maybe the mother who could not express affection in a warm, demonstrative way would hand you a cookie or bake a special dessert for you, handing you a surrogate for an authentic feeling. In marriage, a wife buys scotch for her husband: "Neither he nor I ever have to face things fully." Buddies may insist that everyone join in the "fun" of drinking. These are all ways of making the substances that blank out feelings become a natural part of our lives. Actually, they subvert our natural powers to have fun, to express things with less inhibitions, etc.

The neurotic ego survives on entitlement and control. It believes that it is entitled to have things happen the easy way and, at the same time, wants to be in full control. It is the center and origin of all fear and desire. This neurotic ego fears letting the chips fall where they may, because that means facing surprises and having to be open to all possibilities. It means having to be spontaneous in our responses instead of being in control of them. These substances guarantee (control) how you are going to feel. They are the friends of the neurotic ego. Without these I have to invent creative responses, call upon my courage. I might feel bad all day; I might never wake up fully; I might not be able to relax; I might not be able to fall asleep.

As we saw above, the neurotic ego fears the conditions of existence: I might have to live unprotected and take risks like everybody else! I will look for some distraction and consolation, a psychological D&C! But the healthy adult ego has accepted that there is no one to catch me before I drop and that, furthermore, I do not need anybody to catch me before I drop. I could even land on my bottom, and nothing terrible will happen. I will say "ouch" and get up. There is nobody that has to save me from pain, no godfather necessary to get me through life. I can find solutions within myself. There is no need for mother's little helper for a true adult.

The functional ego has made a commitment to go through everything: to take chances, to seek no refuge, no salve, no easy remedy, no crutches. Substances only serve to keep me helpless, dependent, and afraid. In this sense our work is actually heroic: to live through pain without an anodyne. Our chance at heroism most likely will not be like that of St. Joan of Arc. Our form of heroism will probably be very simple: just to get through the day straight, just to feel what we feel, to take the chance that we may not be fully relaxed or fully awake, etc. Our heroism will be taking back our will and our lives from the distractions and consolations that substances provide.

Our adult task is always to work indefatigably with the ego's tricks using skillful means rather than short-cuts. This is the cold turkey of facing life's challenges. The wonderful thing is that when my ego becomes more adult, that is, lets go of control, lets go of entitlement, lets me feel *this as it is,* I become adept at facing things with full access to my instinctive powers. How does the body join in? Breathe with more depth and openness; sensing your body widening and lengthening to accommodate the freight that faces you, moving with more grace and poise. Then, as Wallace Stevens writes: "It feels good as it is, without the giant...."

Another D&C is "we." Being in relationship may mean running to a partner whenever anything threatening happens to have her/him take care of it for you. This is the godfather relationship! You could use "we-ness" as a way of not having to take care of yourself anymore. The clinging dependency on a partner and the long, plaintive phone conversations with a patient friend about your drama are examples. Healthy people share their feelings directly with the people involved and tell their story to friends in order to process and let go of it. They do not use others to siphon off their own distress and to thereby grant them just enough relief so that no final resolution is necessary. Not only substances, but people and activities can be siphons of feeling. One of our primal needs is the need to be held by our parents. If it was not fulfilled adequately, we might now seek it through frantic sex. But what if, instead, we were to allow ourselves to be held by mother nature. The nature of what? The nature of reality.

What if the methods you use are positive and life-enhancing such as exercise, herbal remedies, etc.? If they are being used to stop you from having to feel the full brunt of something, then there is no distinction between positive and negative. The issue here is what is it being used for and the compulsive and habitual nature of it.

You abandon yourself when, instead of trusting your own powers, you use substances or people as substitutes for them. When you stay with what is, you notice how your body cooperates. You start letting go with more ease. You start having more wisdom and you start noticing that your old limitations are loosening: *limitations that were kept in place by the old escapes.* Once the old evasions are gone, the limitations start to go too. That is the encouraging paradox.

This wonderful quote from the Upanishads fits here, "Curving back within myself, I create again and again and again." I came back to myself and I found a way to create; to become new; to be renewed again and again. Where did I find this? Curving back within myself is how it happens. Turning to a glass of wine or a cigarette is how it does not happen.

Marsilio Ficino, a Florentine philosopher of the Renaissance, says, "Things that enchant us are magical decoys. Only love makes eternity available to mortality." Substances and habits are the magical decoys that do not make anything reliably available but only keep you coming back for more. Anything that keeps you coming back for more is something that could never satisfy you because even too much will not be enough. We have something inside ourselves that works so wonderfully and yet we do not trust it. It is understandable that we do not trust it because for so many years we have disavowed it and denied it. What is the "it"? Our own lively energy, powers that move through us and move us. Like the spider you will meet in Walt Whitman's poem on page 70, you have endless filament to cross your next abyss.

> *If this be our condition, thus to dwell*
> *In narrow circuit straitened by a foe,*
> *Subtle or violent, we not endued*

Single with like defense wherever met,
How are we happy, still in fear of harm?
—*Paradise Lost*, Book IX

TO DO: HOLDING THE FEELING

Here is a simple program: when a fear or any feeling strikes you, stop in your tracks and let it happen; let it go all the way though you and go to ground, like a lightning bolt through a lightning rod. Anything that moves will never hurt you. If it stops in you, then it festers, and destroys you. If you let it move through, it will go to ground, i.e., back to nature. Let the e-motion happen, let it move you forward; let it move out. You do not have to do anything; it wants to happen. It wants to clear itself. It wants to move through. It does not want to remain stuck. This is riding in the direction the horse is going, with the wind at your back.

Every single feeling, including the fear of aloneness, if experienced fully, is ultimately a form of bliss, because every single feeling turns on the lively energy that is inside you. When a feeling reaches its climax of expression, in its bell-shaped curve, it heads toward repose. With this sense of repose is the self-esteem-building realization that you lived through it.

TO DO: IN THE HOUSE OF THE HEALTHY PSYCHE

A mandala is a four-sided or circular figure that represents and enacts the wholeness of the psyche. It is originally a Tibetan image but is found in all cultures and appears in dreams. It can be drawn, danced, or even acted out. The mandala is a meditation device, a way of contemplating the wholeness of the self/universe. Jung says: "It is an attempt at self-healing on the part of nature, which does not spring from conscious reflection but from an instinctive impulse... Mandalas lead us to the inner sacred precinct which is the source and goal of the psyche and contains the unity of life and consciousness...There is no linear evolution; there is only a circumambulation of the Self....The mandala is a picture of this circumambulatory process. It is found in all cultures because of a transconscious disposition in every individual which is able to produce the same or similar symbols at all times and in all places."

Since this mandala wholeness is centered in the unconscious, the archetypal Self is its cause. The ego thrives on a continual relay between desire and fear. We find our true inner direction in the mandala, the wheel of wholeness. It is a compass that transcends the plans we make and the goals we set.

Your healthy mind, which includes every cell of your body, is like a clean, quiet room. It is presided over by you: a healthy ego within a spiritual self, and never by anyone or anything else. The house is the universe with all its living beings and lively events—since there is no inside/outside between self and world!

In this room, there are no screams of terror or horror and no unfulfillable longings, shame, or regrets banging on the walls. Nor are there graffiti on the walls: "You should or should have, you won't, you can't."

Your room often has visitors but it is not haunted by archaic ghosts or current obsessions. Nor is it cluttered by old grudges or new compulsions. Fear and attachment pass through like hikers that take nothing and leave nothing behind. Grief passes as normal since losses happen in this living room. Yet, this is usually a joyous and welcoming room from which you do not seek to flee but in which you find sanctuary and out of which you gather much to give.

This spacious room is not closed in but has four picture windows:

East: rising sun: what is starting to happen and you are taking hold of.

West: setting sun: what is ending and you are letting go of.

North: north star: the stabilizing spiritual force that you live by, i.e., sane and wise love.

South: sunny exposure: your lively energy, imagination, and free-spirited spontaneity.

In the center is an unconditional yes to humanity and spirituality.

Each of us is a universe that wants to expand in every direction.

Your quiet room becomes noisy east and west when you fear or resist the dawn of present challenges or the dusk of necessary endings.

It is noisy north when you have not found a spiritual foundation in yourself.

It is noisy south when you block your potential, hold back your love, or run from it.

A way of knowing a relationship is healthy is that you do not have to shut any windows to be in it.

Who opened my windows? Who closed them? Who showed me where my windows were?

Draw this mandala room and write in the events and choices that fit each window and what is happening for you in each of the four directions of your life right now. *To which are you saying Yes?*

It is a custom at an Indian Mass to place eight flowers in the form of a compass on the altar. This makes the altar the center of the universe. Where would I place my eight flowers?

USE THIS AFFIRMATION: I open myself to all that awaits me: I am defenseless and resourceful in the face of all that may come my way.

FEAR OF ALONENESS

A noiseless patient spider
I marked where on a little promontory it stood isolated,
Marked how to explore the vacant vast surrounding,
It launched forth filament, filament, filament, out of itself.
Ever unreeling them, ever tirelessly speeding them.
And you, O my soul, where you stand
Surrounded, detached, in measureless oceans of space,
Ceaselessly musing, venturing, throwing, seeking the spheres to
      connect them.
Till the bridge you will need be formed, till the ductile anchor hold,
Till the gossamer thread you fling catch somewhere, O my soul!
      —Walt Whitman

Contemplate that scene. The spider looks across the great gap that has no bridge. Instead of being overwhelmed by the seeming impossibility of crossing it, he launches forth from something within himself. He creates a bridge from his own lively energy, "his yarn of pearl," as Emily Dickinson describes it. He rides his own energy across the great abyss to reach the other side. The poem says, "In our souls is filament, filament, filament," plenty to get through life, quite enough to face any eventuality. The bridge we require will be found inside and it has endless length. We can even trust that this gossamer thread that we throw out will catch somewhere! This poem confirms our lively energy and trusts that we have adequate inner yarn (psychological resources) to traverse across any great divide. That is where we begin when we talk about the terror of aloneness.

The worst part of the fear of being alone is the belief that there is no filament—not enough inside me—to launch out and create a bridge. That is the real meaning of the sense of isolation in the neurotic fear of aloneness. Within this is the belief that there must be something wrong with me. "I am alone because I have nothing to offer anyone." Fear of aloneness hearkens to early childhood deficiencies in mirroring. We learned to doubt that potential inside ourselves in our early life when no one mirrored back a trust in our strength. People who, in their childhood, were totally controlled by their parents may have learned that the only way to survive was to be obedient. Alice Miller says, "How can someone taught to obey, ever face the prospect of life alone without a sense of emptiness?"

The sense of loneliness is much more likely when you were told in childhood that your feelings did not matter, a direct attack upon your lively energy. Loneliness will also be more likely if you were continually sent away, even sent to your room, when you were "bad." You may have learned to associate being isolated with not being okay. "When they do not like me they isolate me; therefore, when I feel isolated I am unliked and unlikable." You are also more likely to be lonely if in your childhood there were long periods of boredom and lack of stimulation, when your parents left you to your own devices rather than providing an atmosphere to enliven your powers or activate your potential.

The filaments deteriorate if in the course of the years you never worked on mirroring yourself, i.e., adult self-nurturance. For instance, a person who has handled aloneness by addictive, clinging relationships or addictive substances may thereby have lost access to the filaments inside. Fear of asserting oneself or even of acting in accord with one's deepest needs and wishes, i.e., being oneself, may ultimately be this fear of aloneness. "They will abandon me for this...."

When aloneness is added to fear, the result is loneliness. The element of isolation is precisely where the fear originates. Loneliness happens when you add the belief to aloneness: I cannot really take care of myself. A relationship may become a place to hide. "I do not have any fear of intimacy, I need a relationship." Underneath that "courage" could be: "I am so afraid of being alone I always have to be a 'we,' to have some other arm to lean on."

Any one of these beliefs might lurk within the fear of aloneness:

I am alone because no one wants me;

No one wants to be with me;

I have nothing to offer;

There is nothing I can do about this;

I am totally powerless;

It is never going to get any better;

I feel less than other people who are able to live their life happily;

I am being confined;

I am not in control of my feelings;

I may feel sad;

I may feel fear and be devastated by it

or not be able to do anything about it.

A sense of isolation can occur when you interpret actions as interactions. For instance, you walk into a room where your partner is reading a book and she does not raise her eyes to look at you. She just keeps reading. You interpret her lack of acknowledgment to mean: "She does not care about me; I do not matter; I do not even warrant her raising her eyes from her book." The sense of loneliness comes from this fear or belief. I feel rejected, isolated, and lonely. Obviously, the loneliness you feel in a relationship is much more severe than the loneliness you feel when you are single because of the added element of being rejected by somebody from whom you expected nurturance. *Could it be that I am not as interesting as Charles Dickens?* Erik Erikson asks: "Why do we think the face has turned away which only looked elsewhere?"

Psychologically speaking, my adult identity has an inner core of unlimited lively energy, the psychological boundaries of which I know and I protect; the spiritual boundaries of which are infinite. No boundaries, spiritually, and healthy boundaries, psychologically, ground this inner core of liveliness. That is myself—with just as much thread as a spider!

If you were to begin with the energy inside you, you would locate that same vibrancy that is in the noiseless, patient spider. In fact, every rose and every dragonfly are doing the same thing. They are all joyously living from this lively core that they protect and that at the same time needs no protection. But if your approach is, "I am incomplete and I am needy for someone, or for some thing to make me whole," then there is no hope of ever finding those filaments within, waiting to be found.

A sad double-irony emerges. The first irony is: I am isolated from the outside but there is no outside! Existence is one simultaneous experience. I am connected whether I know it or not. It is an illusion that everything is so separate. The other irony is that we find it within only *when* we confront our own emptiness. The long, lonely night is a prelude when you stay with it and simply allow yourself to notice the emptiness rather than run from it. There is a reliable energy inside which is invisible and yet you do not find it very easily because it is not an "it." It is not even inside because there is no inside or outside. It is something that you are in, as a blade of grass is in something—in a whole atmosphere—and this whole atmosphere is wholly connected. The belief in isolation, therefore, does not quite fit; it is man-made, it is not nature-made.

Chosen solitude has a sense of unlimited connectedness, the very opposite of loneliness in which there is no connection. A monk who believes that his meditations are benefiting the world around him has a sense of connectedness with the world, not a sense of isolation. His solitude is a joyous, not a lonely experience.

To Do: How Loneliness Goes

As with any fear, the adult has a program to deal with aloneness. He is not simply frozen by it. The program is experiencing the aloneness without defense and then finding resources in oneself and in the world to expand one's focus.

To deal with loneliness, a good rule of thumb is to stay with yourself; do not abandon yourself. Mirror yourself by trusting yourself. Stay one more minute than you can stand, increasing the time each day. That one more minute will increase your power exponentially. Unconditional love of yourself is loving yourself when you feel the worst. "Work" also includes: grieving losses, acting assertively, acting with integrity while making choices that follow your bliss. When you do those things you locate your real mettle, your character. All this creates a sense of completeness.

Jung once said, "There is no loneliness, only ever-increasing all-ness." You are all yourself when you let yourself feel all your feelings. Jung also says, "As we wander in the mazes of the psyche, we come upon a secret joy that reconciles us to our path. We find not deadly boredom but an inner partner. When we stand alone, a companion appears." When you finally stand alone as yourself, a companion appears, spiritual or corporeal. An inner partnership begins to happen between yourself and your world. This connectedness contravenes the isolation of loneliness. Connectedness to the universe is St. Thomas' definition of spirituality!

Any time I act in new ways, I run the risk of being disappointed or losing what I was holding on to. *Within every loss is a correlative process by which I can handle it.* That is what is so wonderful about us. Every possible thing that could happen to us has within it the correlative—balancing—possibility of coming to terms with it. For example, if a loss has happened, I can open my grief program-capacity and work it through. Grief involves abandonment. Something or someone has abandoned you. Griefwork brings the balance: you do not abandon yourself. You do not leave but stay with your feelings, as you stay with a child who tells you his nightmare over and over again. The work is just this tender.

TO DO: WORKING WITH LONELINESS, NOT AGAINST IT

The dragon of loneliness suddenly appears and wants to control me. This loneliness is the longing for mirroring (unconditional acceptance) and affiliation that I missed out on long ago. Loneliness is resident pain in my psyche. It is an abandonment fear that has been in me all my life. It is a wilderness only I can cross on the demanding trek to my adulthood.

A face of someone I miss—or a wish for company—arises between the dragon and me. When I thus think of someone as my St. George, I am avoiding my dragon. The solution is, paradoxically, not in a rescuer but in an unconditional acceptance of the loneliness itself, allowing it a full unobstructed track to run its course in me. I then feel my own vulnerability safely because, by taming the dragon on my own, I am empowering myself in a nurturant way.

The loneliness itself is actually the signal of a wound that is already healing since I am finally feeling it, i.e., allowing it into consciousness, the only place where the fear in it can be truly faced and befriended.

My unconscious assumption is that I cannot survive without this other person, or sex, or a new partner, etc. When I make the assumption conscious—and even vocalize it—its absurdity is revealed and my neediness is reduced. In all my relationships, I may have been trying to armor myself against the dragon's charge by interposing someone else's body between me and it!

When I think literally that you are what I need, I am going for the lowest stakes: soothing, distraction, immediate relief. Your absence is not the true source of my pain nor would your presence be freedom from the pain. It would only go underground, into my unconscious, the only place in which it can truly hurt me!

The dragon survives and derives its power from unconsciousness. It bows to me and diminishes to puppy-size when I relate to it in this frank and courageous way. When I fear or am ashamed of my loneliness, I am hiding the most precious, tender, and winsome part of myself behind frantic attempts to become invulnerable. I slap my own face and think I am protecting myself.

There are false beliefs behind that slap (each a blow to my self-confidence):

Re myself: This loneliness is so scary I may die. I will shrivel up because of it. I am helpless in the face of it. No one loves me or wants me or ever will.

Re the other: Without you, there is no me. I cannot be me without you. (When I already know your inadequacy, and still want you as the answer, I am settling for even less: "This is the best I can do, all I deserve.")

The healing work is simple: I stay with my loneliness, i.e., I hold my feelings in a cradling way. I whisk away the conditioned response of anyone else's face and keep coming back to what I am feeling in my body right now. I defang the spiteful grimace loneliness makes at me when I gaze into it and stay with it this way. In such self-mirroring, I speak to myself as the good parent to the child: "I know you are hurting and that you want him now, and yes, it does feel good to be with him. But he cannot really heal your pain. You already tried that many times and it did not work. Now try being with yourself just one more minute than you can stand. One long look is all it takes to diminish, exponentially, both your daunting dragon and his seductive face!" Freud tells us of the beautiful result: "How bold we become when we feel we are loved!"

Longing is perfectly legitimate and a lively part of any sensitive person's experience. It shows the gap between what I want and what I do not have. By owning my own longings—as I own my loneliness—I choose to deepen my sense of its force and frustration. This brave and honest mirroring of longing makes it more livable. As I no longer fear or feel ashamed of my longings, I esteem myself for allowing vulnerability in myself—and letting it be known. Only then do I find out what I really want and am free to be vulnerable *while* owning my power.

My work is not to be free of the need for you but to give to myself first. Then I do not demand or crave or beg but simply ask you to be with me. This liberating truthfulness teaches me how to give to you in return. I pause between the stimulus of my loneliness and the response of longing for your presence. Thereby, I strengthen myself in the skills of intimacy, one of which is accepting the times between us when you may not comfort me but still love me.

With each successful immersion in the self-mirroring of loneliness and longing, new capacities to feel begin opening in me and I become an autonomous adult—the only kind of adult that can love. This happens because I take care of my loneliness by tolerating it alone rather than running to someone else to fill it. I stop holding onto you so dependently and instead, begin, interdependently, to hold you—as I am learning to hold myself. Abandonment has become at-one-ment.

Celeste

Celeste is thirty-five and has never been in a relationship for more than a year. She is so afraid of being abandoned that she clings to a partner for dear life. No matter how much time a man wants to spend with her, she wants more. Celeste believes that all his time belongs to her. This belief emerges from her fear of being alone. She does not hold a partner; she strangleholds him. As soon as a man realizes how tightly she holds on, he leaves her. Her presence feels like a demand rather than a pleasure. Time with her is felt as an obligation rather than a choice.

Celeste also fears that a man in a relationship with her will be unfaithful to her. She watches him in public and wonders about his whereabouts in private. If her obsession becomes strong, she will drive by his house at three or four in the morning to be sure his car is in his driveway. The man in question does not realize this is happening but he does feel pressured by the paranoia that he feels from Celeste generally.

Once, while Celeste was in yet another relationship that was headed for a break-up, she began suspecting that Talbot, her partner, was about to give up on her fairly soon. Her fear became so strong that she became desperate for a solution. She knew that Talbot was low on money and she offered him a rather substantial loan. She was attempting to bribe him but did not see it that way. Talbot was not a man of integrity. He knew the motivation for the loan and knew he could easily take advantage of Celeste's neediness. He accepted the loan and left her within the month. Talbot had no intention of paying her back either!

Meanwhile, Celeste's work was suffering these many months and she was fired. She was now thoroughly devastated. She had given Talbot her life savings and now had no job, no money, and no boyfriend. She felt the fear of dying of isolation in a more real way than ever. Celeste contemplated suicide. She had come to the end of her strategies and had nowhere to turn.

But there was something in Celeste that was stronger than fear: her ego. She began to feel anger not only at herself for her victimizing herself but toward Talbot and all the men she felt had victimized her too. She decided to take action in a new way. Instead of trying to get Talbot back or to find another man, as was her wont, she hired a lawyer. He helped her design a suit to bring against Talbot for the return of her money. It was successful and he agreed to a plan to pay her monthly. For the first time, she had a sense of her own power, not so much because of the success of her suit as for the fact that she no longer wanted Talbot so badly. In fact, for now, she did not want any man!

Celeste surprised herself by this turnaround. In fact, all her friends were surprised too. They had never known Celeste to be without a man or seeking a man. It was hard to believe that this would last. What the friends of Celeste and Celeste herself did not know was that she had found her own power and that had become more appealing to her than any man.

3.

Confronting the Void

Emptiness can mean either vacancy or spaciousness. The Zen monk has a sense of spaciousness and of presence that is not negative and fearsome but positive, joyous, and fearless. Where is the place of fearlessness inside of us? It is exactly in the empty space that we fear as if it were vacancy. Paradoxically, the very thing that we fear is the thing that could move us into freedom from fear.

The sense of vacancy leads to two experiences: loneliness and worthlessness. These equal low self-esteem. Spaciousness and solitude with a sense of connectedness leads to a sense of inner worth, because I am perfect without having to do anything. The worth is within (like the filaments) rather than in what I accomplish. Since "nature abhors a vacuum," I am going to have to fill it in with drama, with storylines, with addictions. It seems as if I am filling in my empty space, but actually I am creating a hole.

Within solitude and inner worth, all that happens is receptiveness to whatever may come our way, an unconditional yes to that which is and will be. Instead of it being a hole, it is wholeness: I with all, all in me. Within the drama and the story, all I am doing is holding on for dear life to all the things that seem to fill me. When I am receptive, I am not holding on. I have a sense of being held by the universe, the posture of spirituality.

A SENSE OF EMPTINESS

Within the human condition of aloneness is the possibility of confronting a void, a dark inner sense of unremitting emptiness. The Apocalypse says: "When the seventh seal was opened, there was silence in heaven for about a half hour." That silence in heaven, when no voice speaks to you no matter how hard you try to hear it, is the void. It is a spiritual fear because it transcends life, death, and human remedy. The possibility of converting the emptiness into spaciousness cannot happen in the void. You have access only to the emptiness. The void defies our will and intellect as well as our spiritual practices. The sense of a total loss brings up a panic-striking fear of abandonment. You feel you are being abandoned by the universe and by any higher power you may believe in. In other words, the void is the loss of all your supports, visible and invisible. Everything that used to work for you no longer works. It feels like a cancellation of your connectedness.

If prayer works to get you out of the void, then it is not the void. If activity works to get you out of the void, then it is not the void. If someone can fix you, then it is not the void. If substances work, it is not the void. In fact, if anything works, it is not the void. This is the point in life when nothing works. The experience of the void can happen once or any number of times in the course of one's life. It can last an hour or a decade.

From the Jungian perspective, the void is the challenge to integrate the orphan archetype. Each of us has an orphan inside, an unparented, exposed, abandoned, child. It is something in us that nobody wants, that nobody will take care of, or even hold. Somehow we find ourselves in a position of having nobody who can fix things for us; nobody who can gather us up and carry us away from the dreadful emptiness. This is a legitimate archetype of the human unconscious—a condition of our cosmic existence. It asks to be faced and integrated.

The experience of the void can demolish self-esteem because I may imagine: "Something is terribly wrong with me. This is happening because of something I have done," or "I have no resources; I can't fight this." Yet inability to fight and conquer is a legitimate, psychologically appropriate thing sometimes! Simply to face emptiness in life for a minute or an hour or a month or a year and not be able to handle it is our right. This is the point in the journey at which you are not supposed to be able to deal with what faces you. Sometimes the hero has to deal with the dragon: fight it, kill it, and then there are other times when he cannot deal at all. He falls and things seem hopeless for a while. Robin Hood is not in Sherwood now, but helpless in the dungeon. The void imprisons us in just such a moment.

Psyche, on her journey, was unable to sort out the grains of Aphrodite. Ants came from deep in the earth and did the task for her. The void cannot be sorted out; all we can do is trust the earth—which may not go to work as quickly for us as it did for her.

The void is not another way of talking about depression. This is a spiritual event/crisis in the life of the psyche. It is a true silence, like the silence that Jesus experienced on three occasions. It happened first when he was in the desert and he met the Shadow. Secondly, in the Garden of Gethsemane, he foresaw what he would have to suffer. He asked the disciples to support him, to help him get through this blood-sweat night, and they fell asleep—no voice from heaven and no support from earthly friends. Nothing worked. The third, and worst of all, was on the cross when he said, "Why hast thou forsaken me?" In the void is the sense of forsakenness: "I have been abandoned here, left behind, orphaned of man and God, and nobody will come to take care of me or care about me." In that final forsaken silence, he knew the fullness of humanity. It takes at least one void to grant us the red badge of humanness.

In the void there is a free fall with no possibility of finding a foothold. There is nothing to grab onto, no leg up. You cannot get a handle on your experience and there seems to be no end in sight. A poem by Emily Dickinson starts with the words, "Pain has an element of blank. It cannot recollect when it began or if there were a time when it was not." To this silence there seems to be no end, in this darkness no light. If you could convince yourself that there were a light at the end of the tunnel, it would not be the void.

"Is this a phase that I am going through?" Your mind will not take refuge in that. Your mind only believes: "I am here in this desolate silence and it is not going to end." Your greatest fear, in fact, is that you will not die! The void has been called "the dark night of the soul" or "the encircling gloom." It is not quite aloneness; it is not quite loneliness; it is more than desperation, despair, or isolation. It is all of those, times one hundred.

What is going on? The ego is confronting the inadequacy of its two main pillars—control and entitlement. The neurotic ego wants to be in full control—to avoid the possibility of not getting what it wants. My ego also represents the belief that I am entitled to be taken care of and to be loved by everyone. In this experience of the void, both of these are cancelled because: "I have no control over this and I do not feel as if I am entitled to be rescued from it." *The ego is discovering its actual condition:* it is not really solid, able, or strong enough to face every eventuality. It has no real ground; it has no real basis. In fact, there is nothing inside me that is a separate identity with power. What is really in here is a no-thing, a space, a void—as Zen always said. Is my inner core of identity a fiction? The void says: "Yes and it is time you knew it."

The ego is in panic because of the possibility of egolessness. If I let go of the control and the entitlement which make up myself, I will be egoless. The deepest spiritual fear is of

losing one's identity, of having no real sense of being somebody. This is precisely what happens in the void. "If I let go of
control over my partner or my children, I will not be anybody." In the scared ego, letting go is equated with annihilation. It is the spiritual stair that is not there.

In ancient times, this sense of panic was associated with
nature. Pan is the God of Nature, and our word "panic" is a
derivative of his name. In later Christian times, Pan, who had
horns and a tail, was turned into the devil. Behind this lurked
the belief that nature cannot be trusted and that nature will
drop you into chaotic terror. It is a denial that *chaos is a legitimate phase in our evolution.* This is ultimately a denial of creativity since the Spirit brooded on the waters of chaos to form
the universe! We oppose and control nature. Yet it, like the
void, cannot be controlled, nor is it necessary.

Here and now I could be in the void and think of it as a
horse to ride—although a ghostly pale horse. That would be
a yes to the frightening side of nature, my own underworld
come up to haunt me. Or I could say yes to ego and beat a
dead horse. I could fight this absolute emptiness and iden-
titylessness. Then something very strange happens: I notice
that I am so afraid I cannot even defend myself. I cannot think
of a solution. My mind does not work. My defense mechanisms do not work. No insights. No enlightenment. No
favorite sayings. No consolations. Nothing works. This helpless ego is having a direct vision of its ultimate condition: "I
am a king of shreds and patches."

All my strategies in life have merely patched me
together so that I could make it through the day without having to face my void. Now I have to look at the darkest corners
of this and my existence and fail at finding something that
will save me. *Have I been using everything, even my faith, as
avoidances of the void?*

For the first time I see just how fraudulent, puny, and
ultimately unreliable my ego really is: Even the authenticity
of my love for my partner, or my love for my family, or for

God, I now question. I notice more clearly how in every one of these areas there is an unworthy motive that makes me not quite the person I thought I was. I do not seem to have the integrity that I thought I had. I do not seem to know what I thought I knew. Everything is called into question and I see my shadow. I impugn myself and my self-esteem comes even more to naught as panic closes in.

Our fortress against emptiness was and is really only a house of cards, and it easily disperses in the vastness of this chasm that opens up before us and which no bridge can span. We are plunging into the abyss with no chance of finding a way out and with no life preserver thrown in after us. Even the sources that used to be so good at throwing one to us fail us now. Francis Thompson in his poem, *The Hound of Heaven,* says: "Aye, faileth now even dream the dreamer and lute the lutanist...even the linked fantasies are yielding: cords of all too weak account...." Things are no longer holding, things are no longer able to do what they used to do. The resourceful ego itself, with all its tricks and charms, lies exsanguinated in this dread plot.

I begin to realize, for the first time, that security is my *occasional* condition, not my permanent condition. Security really means, "I am succeeding in staving off the possibility of having to face my inner void." I have feared a direct vision of my ultimate condition without the usual, trusty succor that has helped me avoid it. Everything I had held onto, all the things I had to be in control of, all my entitlements, all my ambitions, all my claims on fame and fortune—all were ways of protecting myself from having to free-fall into this void. The habits, the bulwarks, the dramas and all the people that I thought of as my support system were stationed between me and this fear that I would somehow have to surrender my ego. This opens up all the griefs of my life that have been hidden by my having been in control.

It is not as if the healthy ego was meant to be killed off. We have to maintain our functional ego in order to cross the street. We are looking here at the neurotic ego, now having to unmask itself as the great pretender.

The presiding god over the dissolution of the ego is the trickster, part of the shadow archetype, the joker who humorously or cunningly shows us just how inadequate we are. In *Richard II*, Shakespeare describes the trickster sitting near the royal throne: "Within the hollow crown that rounds the mortal temples of the king, keeps death his court. And there the antic sits, scoffing his state and grinning at his pomp, allowing him a little breath to monarchize, be feared and kill with looks...." That is being in control and being entitled. "As if this flesh which walls about our life were brass-impregnable." We thought we had the power to go on forever in that controlling state. "And humored thus, comes at the last (the trickster comes at last after having humored the ego into believing its own pretenses) and with a little pin bores through his castle wall and farewell king." Somehow the trickster breaks through and breaks open this neurotic ego part of ourselves.

I teach at a college and have the use of a copier. One day I went to the copy machine and punched in my correct identification number as I had done many times before, but this time instead of saying "go for it," it said "Invalid Account." The machine was saying I no longer had a recognizable identity. So I punched in the same set of numbers again and the same message came up "Invalid Account." There was no way to convince it otherwise. The combination that had worked a hundred times before now no longer worked.

Now I am nobody with no remedy. There is no one to turn to. And I am of no account. It is not saying I have exceeded my quota of copies or that I do not have the power to do what I want; it is saying there is no me, there is no such person with that number.

This seems to me like a metaphor for the void because that is exactly what happens in it. You are given the impression that this recognizable identity is no longer recognizable. You cannot prove your existence.

I did not mind having my identity canceled, my power denied, but I did want the copies! The only thing I could do was to report it to the authorities, and there is where the analogy breaks down because when you are in the void you have no one to report it to. No recourse. It is the court of last appeal where no appeals are possible. You punch in the same old tricks and same old methods that used to work to get you through little depressions and panic attacks, but this time they do not work. They have become invalid, useless. You are void of effective techniques; you are voided; you are in a void.

VOID OF EGO

Void, then, really means void of ego with all its protective devices and boundaries. The very thing that hurts so much could be the exact replica of the inner, invisible world, where there are no boundaries, where there is no identity, and where there is also no need to be in control. This void could be telling me about my real identity which is pure boundarylessness. I am just out there in space and everything else in my life is filler. *Could this mean that everything I have called a support could be a limiting wall around me?*

The void has brought me to the gateway of myself in this very strange, dark, and spiritually canny way. *This fear of the empty space is what ego really is.* The empty space is what we really are. Fear has made us fill it in with every possible distraction and consolation that works to cancel it. Or another way of saying it is: "I fear being myself when myself means not being in control. I am afraid of unconditional being. I want the existence that is conditioned by my little habits and fenced by my little safe places to run to." Instead, here is an escapeless confrontation with unconditional being. *In a contemplative way can I allow myself to stay with it and to open myself to this information which has been tabooed until now?*

The void is like the Tibetan concept of a "bardo." "Bar" means "between" and "do" means "suspended." What a fascinating phrase! In neither one of them is there something to grab onto. You cannot grab onto "between" and you cannot grab onto "suspended." Bardos are the phases that we pass through as we die. We can apply these to the death of ego. We are "suspended between" ego and nature. This gap between the completion of one thing and the commencement of another has become all that remains of us, all that we really are.

In this suspended state, the false pretenses and the defenses—neither of which are willing or able to help me— have collapsed. Here I am suspended now, between nothing and nothing. Emily Dickinson's poem about a spider says: "He plies from naught to naught...." That empty space calls for no special movement: just stay there with it. The image of the Buddha sitting under the tree or of Christ crucified on the cross is an image of this suspended point in the journey when simply to stay is all that is required or possible.

The void is like a gap, but not totally, since a gap exists between two definite points. I was married before, and plan to be married again, but now I am in the gap between mar- riages. The void does not feel like this kind of a gap because there is no place from which you had jumped and there is no place to which you are jumping. In fact, there is even a doubt about whether there is someone to do the jumping!

One might hope that the gap is something like a move- ment from the death of ego to a reborn state where the func- tional ego will find an axis with the true self for spiritual and psychological wholeness. Instead, by entering into the void, something has died and there is no secure connection to something that might be better. This is why it is not a gap but a void.

Are we on our way to a tomb, which will be the end of us, or are we on our way to a womb, which will be the con- tainer for the beginning of a new life? It is the same question we ask about the grave. We have no answer. In fact, the proper spiritual etiquette during this void seems to be simply not knowing. I do not know whether I am going to new life or to death. Emily Dickinson says: "Uncertain of the length of this that is between, it goads me like the goblin bee that will not state its sting." It will not tell me what I cannot know. It

will not tell me what it is about, this no-place of unknownness
in which I cannot know.

I entered I knew not where,
And there I stood not knowing:
Nothing left to know...
                                             —St. John of the Cross

THE VOID CALLS

I have a journey, sir, shortly to go.
My master calls me; I must not say no.
The weight of this sad time we must obey...
                                             —*King Lear*

In the spiritual view the void is also presided over by the
Holy Spirit that brooded over the original waters of chaos to
bring about the creation. The Holy Spirit is the female power,
counterpoised to the trickster—male energy. The female dove
broods over the unhatched young in order to bring them to
life. During this gap, the old is dying but the new has not yet
been born and our limited consciousness does not even know
if it will be born.

If we come through to the other side, to the experience of
rebirth, now free of what we realize are the shackles of the
ego, we are in the arms of the gods of resurrection, Christ,
Osiris, Dionysus. They preside over the emergence of this
new self. It could happen through a sudden release or
through a series of steps and shifts—like all enlightenments.
From the Gnostic perspective, which led in medieval times to
alchemy, it is an "Anima Mundi"—a spirit of the world, that
creates form but still remains in matter. The alchemical work
was to release the divine from the matter. When the Holy
Spirit broods over the chaos, she not only brings it to life but
she leaves her life in it. The spiritual work is to free divinity

from matter, to find the spiritual in nature. It is just the opposite of the fear of nature!

The first part, the death of ego, corresponds to Good Friday. On that Friday, Christ said: "This is your hour in the power of darkness," i.e., darkness is a legitimate part of the journey. The ultimate end, hopefully, will be an Easter Sunday. Between is Holy Saturday, lying still in the tomb. And we do not know how long this Saturday will last.

> *And though the last lights off the black west went,*
> *Oh, morning at the brown brink eastward, springs—*
> *Because the Holy Ghost over the bent*
> *World broods with warm breast and with ah! bright wings.*
> —Gerard Manley Hopkins

The void, from the perspective of the hero's journey, could also be the point of the call. Only those who are ready to hear this call would ever be invited into this strange place. Because in this place you would ultimately discover, after simply having stayed with it, that you have an enormous potential, that is not yet actualized. The destination is that richer side; the way there is suspension in the void.

This Zen blow was only the thud of landing on your true reality: I am not in control; everything could fall apart; everything that worked could stop working and I will just be out there, and I will not know whether I am on my way to rebirth or to an even worse crucifixion. Thomas Merton calls this "the deep existential crisis that precedes the final integration of the self." Jonah goes into the dark place inside the whale—his own unconscious—thinking he will never come out and then he is hurled back out onto the shore with a new sense of purpose. Or it could be that we are an alchemical vessel and that a transformation is happening in this crucible-void? Joseph Campbell says, "It's a void because we can't reach it or outreach it." All we can do is adjust ourselves to its midnight.

STAYING IN SUSPENSE: NOTHING TO DO:

Entering into the utmost emptiness, I maintain the still-
ness wholeheartedly.

—Lao Tzu, *Tao* 16

The void is not a place; it is the mind. The only choice for us is staying in suspense. This is suspense in both senses: you are suspended in mid-air, and at the same time you are unclear as to what will happen next. You are not minimizing what is going on as a rationalizer might, not using any rites or formulas as a priest might, not being frozen or possessed by the void, as a psychotic might. You are living in a fierce container: the archetypal Self. If you are embraced by it you are no longer containing it—it is containing you.

I get through by staying in suspense, the same way I got through my mother's pregnancy. Now in the womb of the goddess, mother earth—another metaphor for the void—I simply stay. Sometimes our psychological work is very taxing, like grieving the end of something. Sometimes our work is not so arduous, like learning how to be assertive about something. Here the work is the simplest of all: stay there as opposed to trying to run away from it, and be in suspense as opposed to trying to understand it or change it. It might also be described as something like floating, which is not passive but an active responsiveness to the buoyancy of the water.

This void is total disillusionment, since you come to the end of all your illusions of what would work, of everything that worked before, everything from prayer to personal charms. Once I have experienced total disillusionment, I can never again know despair. We never again know despair because we never again attach ourselves to the possibility that there is something that might always work. We drop that final, childish belief that there is always something that will do it for us, always a way around a given instead of a way through it. We are ready for the bravest human affirmation:

"I let go of more than any fate can take." That is why we can never again be the victims of despair: We have already chosen it! Arjuna felt despair and it soon revealed itself as the precisely shaped vacancy in which Krishna could find hospitality. The two disciples en route to Emmaus found the Everything in the Nothing of their desperation.

Jesus walked into the desert, looking for the void, wanting to be there for forty days and forty nights. The Jews left Egypt, a symbol of ego's blandishments, and traveled in the desert void for forty years. Buddha sat under the Bo tree for six years. Each looked for the emptiness, the exinanition, the emptying out of oneself so that one could be an alchemical vessel. If the void means no control, then the void means no ego. Exinanition is the emptying out of the ego.

The only obstacle to grace—access to a power beyond my own mind or will—is control. Therefore, the void is really the grace of finding out that the ego has nothing to offer when the chips are down. Or another way of saying it is that the void gives you perfect access to grace, the grace of the pause, the blank space, where infinite possibility happens because personal control has wavered.

When I sit in suspense, as Buddha sat under the tree, I am actually fire-walking in my psyche. It scares and burns me. I am dropping all the gestures that were meant to suppress the fear. Not only am I no longer trying to use what could work, I have decided to drop everything and not to try anything else. I am walking through this fire instead of walking around it. I am staying in suspense and the "I" that is staying here is the very center of my psyche—the Self as opposed to the neurotic ego. The Self can swim in the same ocean that would drown the ego. The Self is the center that does not need things centered. We are New England November souls.

As I simply stay, a new vulnerability arises in me, a softness, not a stronger armor. When I tried all the tricks and methods, I was more lost in the void than protected against it.

This is how the trickster tricked me! I was catapulted into the void by chance, and now, sitting in suspense, I change the chance to choice. I have entered the cave that has become a mine, and in this mine are the diamonds of "no mind." It was the mind, the neurotic ego, that kept conjuring, with all its fear and desire, new ways to make things work my way. Virginia Woolf may have been referring to the diamond self when she wrote: "Things are losing their hardness, even my body now lets the light through."

But now I find the diamond, the imperishable, impenetrable, and light-filled indestructible stone of "no mind," in other words, the essence of my star-stuff self. A diamond and a star and I are all one single thing, and I found that out when I simply stayed in the suspense. I am what nature is—transitory and ever-lasting. Like the diamond, I have to allow many centuries of great weight upon me. I have allowed this weight and long pause to occur. The void is the pause from the frantic drama of the ego. It is a pause I had to take at first, and now I choose to take it. When this happens I find something new in it. Finding cannot be my motivation; that is not suspense. The buried treasure may or may not be excavated. But if it is, it will happen to those with no shovels or treasure maps. It happens to those who sit quietly in the dark.

This is the darkness under the cloth during the rising of the dough. It *has* to remain in the dark while the mysterious power of rising occurs. In that pause in the midst of all our usual activities, in that staying in suspense, it comes to life. It does not work if we take the cloth off and look inside. That is the attempt to know, the attempt to control, the attempt to analyze. Instead we simply allow ourselves to be in suspense about whether it will rise or not—depending on how good the yeast and the kneading were—symbols of the gift of nature and the effort of man, the winning combination. We recall that Jung says, "We must be alone to discover what supports us when we can no longer support ourselves. Only aloneness gives us an indestructible foundation." Only in our aloneness have we found the purpose of our work: to allow what wants to happen.

You are not staying in suspense because it works, but because that is the only thing you can do. It is realism; it is not a method. You stay for the same reason that you sit when you meditate. You do not sit and meditate because you are trying to become enlightened. You sit because you sit. If enlightenment happens sometime, that is fine. If it does not happen, that is fine too. Jung adds a sanguine note, "There is in the psyche a process that seeks its own goal no matter what the external factors may be."

The external factors may not look good as you stay in suspense. Your friends may suggest therapy or medication. Letting your world collapse and simply going with it is joining Samson in pushing the pillars aside so that the whole temple of distractions and consolations can collapse. He was allowing everything about ego to fall, letting himself, his "mangled youth, lie dead beneath the heap," as Francis Thompson writes. No one will like the mess you make.

Yes, I want my ego to be crushed in that way.
I accept the void as the final, richest condition of existence.

It is not only a condition of existence. It declares my real identity: the great pretender who struts and postures with all the gestures and poses that are meant to charm away the darkness awaiting me. Meister Eckhart says plainly: "Everything is meant to be lost that the soul may stand in unhampered nothingness." To stand in unhampered nothingness is to stay in suspense. Everything is *meant* to be lost. All the little tricks are meant to fall apart. The total disillusionment is meant to happen. It happened in order that we might stand in nothingness, be in the bardo, suspended and still standing. William Blake says, "I must let go of it all lest the judgment come and find me unannihilate and I be delivered into the hands of my own selfhood." My whole ego is supposed to be dismantled, otherwise I will be the victim of it. St. John of the Cross welcomes this: "Swiftly, with nothing spared, I am being completely dismantled!" The mystic, St. Catherine of Genoa, adds, "My me is God. There is no other I." *Could freedom from fear be the same as letting go of ego?*

> *O Spirit...Thou from the first*
> *Wast present, and, with mighty wings outspread,*
> *Dovelike sat'st brooding on the vast abyss,*
> *And mad'st it pregnant: what in me is dark*
> *Illumine....*
> —Paradise Lost

THE NET

> *...the net whose every knot contains a diamond.*
> —Avatamsaka Sutra

The spider weaves the bridge of pearl from within herself. The trapeze artist flies through the air with a net below. In the healthy ego, in the functional ego, there is a net woven early in life. This net is woven of strands from early experiences of soul-bonding within the holding environment of your family. It comes from the mirroring that came from your mother or father as you showed lively energy. When you have had at least good enough parenting—it does not have to be perfect— there is a net inside your psyche. If you fall, you will fall safely and even bounce. This is how it is for people who were not dropped in childhood. They were not emotionally abandoned but mirrored. Their parents loved them for what they felt and validated what they felt. Every time that happened, a new strand was being woven in their psychic net so that they could believe what the poem says, "There are many arms around us and the things we love." They grew up realizing that they really were loved and that they were permitted to fall and someone would catch them. They could even jump and someone would allow it. They were allowed to separate. They were allowed to individuate. Freedom from fear is an exoneration that began—or did not begin—in childhood.

A baby eagle is pushed out of the nest by its mother. This is how it learns to fly. The father times the arc of its fall as it flaps its wings and tries to become air-worthy. He opens his wide wings and catches his little one on his back just before it hits the ground and then he brings it back up into the nest. The mother pushes the baby out again and the father swoops down, catches, and brings it back up. The father is, in fact, chosen by the mother for his skill at doing this. The height of the nest is gauged by just exactly how long an eaglet will need to fall before it can learn to fly. The whole thing is organized in such a way that it can fall, be caught, and learn to fly at the same time. That is what is meant by soul-bonding. When it has happened for us, we can fall with the trust that there will be a net, a soft fatherly back to land on.

A containing, holding environment leads to a sense of security in adult life. People who, in childhood, received love and nurturance never ultimately fear being lost in the great abyss. They may free-fall but somehow every cell of their psyche, if it were to have cells, trusts: "somehow I will survive this." You may not always have it in your consciousness. You may doubt it a moment here or there, but somewhere inside, you go on trusting: "All I have to do is stick with this and somehow it is all going to work out in some way." The metaphor of the eagle is an apt one because what we are really trusting is nature. We are trusting the natural instinct that mother nature had to help us leave the nest. She knew exactly the right time for each of us and has a back prepared.

If you did miss the weaving of the net in childhood, you can still weave it now by grieving the losses of childhood, working through things in therapy and Twelve-Step programs, and by being loved unconditionally in healthy relationships. It is woven strongly by the fearwork presented in this book.

Successful weaving is ultimately the integration of the orphan archetype, accepting that I am alone in this work and noticing that visitors sometimes come to my gate to offer an embrace. This net will be woven by the healthy person before it is needed. That is working on yourself. The unhealthy person can only weave it after it is needed. That is recovery. The net makes the stagnant void into a fertile void. It is fertile like the desert that produces the redolent blooms that sometimes are not even noticed: "Full many a flower is born to blush unseen/And waste its sweetness in the desert air" as Thomas Gray writes.

This fertility may not be noticed but it is always present. "I notice I do not fall as far." When you hear that statement from someone who has been in the void more than once, you know there is a net inside her. It does not break the fall, it only allows it to happen safely.

A suicidal reaction to a crisis shows you to have no net. When you turn to anorexia, or alcoholism, etc., in a crisis, that shows no net. The borderline personality has no net. If you know that you do not have this net, it is wise not to jump into any abysses or any scary spaces in your psyche. For example, if you have a suspicion that some terrible abuse occurred to you in early life but you also know you do not yet have what it takes to handle it, do not delve into it. It is better to work on your net first.

There are also synthetic nets—cults, addictions, safe, rigid belief systems. When these do not encourage the release of my own powers they are ersatz nets and will not really work. This is what Jung meant when he said, "Religion is a defense against the religious experience." It can become this when it provides a false refuge from the conditions of adult existence, conditions that require us to be defenseless and resourceful if we are to mature.

The void is now revealed fully as the unconditional being that is our true self. *The something within you that allows you to stay is the net.* A new power arises in you: "the sudden surfacing of a strength, that takes you beyond rational expectation or hope" as Durkheim reports. It is not like thinking; it is like nature.

The void is space to grow in. We called it emptiness. Now we are seeing that it is spaciousness, the same kind of space as in the womb. The void is a womb, the womb of the earth mother. It is not a maw in which nothing can be created; it is a womb in which something new is being born, secretly, silently, and scarily. St. Francis in the cave prayed: "Let me hide in the womb of this wet earth that sponges me in soft gentle mud. O womb of earth, hide me from eyes that freeze me in paralyzing fear."

Vainamoinen is the Finnish hero who remained in his mother's womb for thirty years before his birth. In that void he became a magician and a musician. He also learned how to live in the void! All our soul ever wanted was to be born and this is how it happens. Could it be then that forsakenness is necessary, spiritually, as betrayal is necessary, psychologically? Without them, we might never have looked within. We might have trusted only the outside with its toys and decoys, if desolation had not happened. This is the forsakenness that Christ faced on the cross and the one that we face when everything we depend upon falls apart. This forsakenness moves you away from any immature religious clinging in which you were seeking the consolations of God. The consolations of God are gone and all that is left is the God of all consolation who does not always console. The void is the true religious experience: the moment-momentum of the silence of God.

Mircea Eliade says, "The hero gives up completely all attachment to his personal limitations, idiosyncrasies, hopes, and fears. He no longer resists the self-annihilation that is prerequisite to rebirth in the realization of truth, and so becomes ripe, at last, for the great at-one-ment. His personal ambitions being totally dissolved, he no longer tries to live but willingly relaxes to whatever may come to pass in him; he becomes, that is to say, an anonymity. *The Law of life lives in him with his unreserved consent....*The void shows us the inadequacy, the fragility, the bankruptcy of our personality that was born in time. But look how this is actually the very threshold to a spiritual rebirth. The ideal of yoga is to live in an eternal present outside of time, no longer possessing a personal consciousness or history, that is, a consciousness nourished on his own history, but instead a witnessing consciousness which is pure lucidity and spontaneity. It is obtained by death to the human condition and rebirth to a transcendent mode of being. It is anticipating death in order to ensure rebirth in a sanctified life, that is, a life now made real because it includes the sacred."

Buddhism anticipated the reluctant conclusions of modern psychology: guilt and anxiety are not adventitious but intrinsic to the ego. According to my interpretation of Buddhism, our dissatisfaction with life derives from a repression even more immediate than death-terror: the suspicion that "I" am not real. The sense-of-self is not self-existing but a mental construction which experiences its own groundlessness as a lack. This sense-of-lack is consistent with what psychotherapy has discovered about ontological guilt and basic anxiety. We usually cope with this lack by objectifying it in various ways and try to resolve it through projects which cannot succeed because they do not address the fundamental issue.

So our most problematic dualism is not life fearing death but a fragile sense-of-self dreading its own groundlessness. By accepting and yielding to that groundlessness, I can discover that I have always been grounded, not as a self-contained being but as one manifestation of a web of relationships which encompasses everything. This solves the problem of desire by transforming it. As long as we

*are driven by lack, every desire becomes a sticky attach-
ment that tries to fill up a bottomless pit. Without lack,
the serenity of our no-thing-ness, i.e., the absence of any
fixed nature, grants the freedom to become anything.*
—David Loy, *Journal of Transpersonal Psychology,* 92.
Vol. 24, No. 2, p. 176.

4.

When Love Meets Fear

Love bade me welcome yet my soul drew back, guilty of dust and sin. —George Herbert

The modern repression is not of sex but of love. Most of us have early and recent histories of danger and abandonment associated with our giving and receiving of love. We may have erected walls to keep ourselves safe, walls that also keep us from being loved. The fear of being loved can be rationalized as the fear of rejection or of engulfment. Actually, very profound and unhealed wounds in our psyches lurk behind our fears of closeness. Acceptance and love from someone toward us involve an engaged focus on us that may be terrifying. Without a history of safety in being loved, we may never have learned how to receive such affection-bearing attention. We are all able to explore these painful but redeemable territories of our psyche. We can learn the way to let love through or in, and how to approach someone who fears our love. There are specific and gentle techniques that can release the scared ego's hold-outs and hide-outs.

Most of us have been afraid of love all our lives and have never realized it fully. We fear love when we run from commitment, refuse to state that we want to be loved, refuse to hear it said to us, refuse to receive it. What are the rationalizations that may appear when love comes along? "I might be engulfed by the other person. I might lose my freedom. I have to be very careful about protecting my boundaries. I might be so engulfed and smothered by the other person's love that I lose my own identity. The other person might demand or take too much from me. I might be let down. I might be disappointed. I might be rejected. I might be betrayed. I might not measure up." In other words, I might have to face the conditions of existence like everybody else!

We all need and seek love. Love can only be trusted when we are made to feel safe to be ourselves. "I can show you who I am and you will love me." This unconditionality in a trustworthy environment makes us feel safe. Early in life, many betrayals and disappointments may grow up around our wish for love. It becomes difficult to trust those who seem to be our only sources of love when they do not accept us as we are. How paradoxical that later we may not accept ourselves when our work of handling fear requires that we accept ourselves as scared!

It may never have been safe to be yourself in the living room or at the kitchen table. You might have been hit; you might have been made fun of; you might have been intimidated. The only safe place was in your own room alone, or outside, or away. Today there may be an association in your mind between closeness and danger and between distance and safety.

Your body may even carry a recollection of an early intrusion, or abuse, that happened to you in childhood, which is no longer in your conscious memory. Your body still carries the pain and the impact. This interrupts and blockades the natural instinct to welcome love. Now when someone touches you, or holds you, or shows love toward you, it recreates the original abusive scenario and something in your body says, "Do not trust this, pull away, move back, get away." The more shut down a person is, the worse may have been the intrusion and the abuse. The real question is not, "Why are you so shut down?" The real question is, "What must have happened to you to make love so scary?" As Alice

Miller says, "The stronger the prisoner is, the thicker the walls have to be..."

This wall that we began building early in life keeps rising slowly, all through the years. It keeps others out but it also keeps us in. Under it is this doubt: "I will not be able to protect my boundaries; I will not be able to take care of myself in relationship." "I will not be able to say, 'Don't tread on me.'" I fear that I will lose something of myself if I am loved by you.

> *All alone, or in twos, the ones who really love you*
> *walk up and down outside the wall.*
> *Some, hand in hand,*
> *and some gather together in bands.*
> *The bleeding hearts of the artistes take their stand.*
> *And when they have given you their all,*
> *some stagger and fall.*
> *After all, it's not easy*
> *banging your heart against some mad bugger's wall.*
>
> —Pink Floyd

This is the wall that we build so that people will not get too close or love us too much. We watch them walking around and trying to get in. We notice how hurtful it is to them when they cannot get in. Our rational mind keeps excusing us: "That is their business, not mine." The wall that we build has the given purpose of protecting us. But that does not usually happen. Instead, the wall protects the fear. It guarantees that we go on fearing because we stay inside, huddled up, safe but never getting the chance to confront and transcend our fear. *What this wall does is protect the imprisoning fear that is in us.* It does not really protect the true us; it protects the scared us—the one that has the history of abuse or intrusion or mistrust. Fearing love is like being a beggar fearing money. At one and the same time we maintain our fear of love, and still keep looking for it.

The wall we built to keep love out
Will also keep fear in.

FEAR AND LOVE

Fear is a signal by which we notice what we have not yet integrated. For example, you integrate a lake by learning to swim in it! Not integrating it would be standing at the edge and fearing you might drown if you enter it. To be foolhardy and throw yourself off the bridge to make yourself swim will not work either. But if you take lessons and gradually learn to swim, you become able to integrate the challenging reality of water, and you no longer fear it. We fear something that we do not allow into our experience. In this sense, fear is a form of alienation.

Everything in human experience can be integrated along those same lines. Money can be integrated by using it as a tool and not being afraid of earning, spending, saving, giving, receiving, etc. Sex can be integrated by enjoying it without inhibition but with responsibility.

A "problem" in life means that something has not yet been integrated. Integration happens when we address, process, and resolve the problem. If you marry, and as soon as things get rough you have an affair, drink, or leave, the commitment has not been integrated.

Our personality is made up of a combination of opposites. Our challenge is to create synthesis, order from chaos, unity from diversity. If there is fear in us, there must be fearlessness too. If there is violence, there is non-violence. If there is grudge and vengeance, there is compassion and forgiveness. Every characteristic in you has an opposing side, potentially accessible. This hidden side is called the shadow. The shadow is a Jungian term referring to the disowned and hidden parts of ourselves, positively the traits that are admirable and negatively those that are ugly. If you are extremely vengeful in your conscious choices, then in your positive, hidden shadow side there is that same amount of compassion. The more strongly violent you are, the more strongly nonviolent could you be. The more you fear, the more love lies in hiding.

Joseph Campbell said: "The part of us that wants to become is fearless." Your true self is where your fearlessness lives. As long as we are trying to do what other people want us to do, as long as we are afraid of what other people think, we will fear. The fearlessness comes when you make a commitment to be who you fully are. I may abandon myself to prevent others from alienating themselves from me! Instead of saying, "I do not want people to know that I am this way because then they will not like me," I may begin to say, "I want them to know exactly how I am because my commitment is to becoming myself more than to having them like me. I want everybody to know who I really am, so I drop all the poses that I have adopted to look good." A wonderful poise results: fearlessness.

"True love casts out fear." We can see that love and fear are opposites, so fearlessness is another name for love. As fear represents what we have not yet integrated, love is that which integrates everything. It is an unconditional responsiveness to what is rather than a conditioned response to what we have learned. Love is total yes. Fear is no. Love gives us access to the unconditional being that is our endless potential. Since our spiritual destiny is to release the riches of the Self— unconditional/universal love, perennial wisdom, and healing power—through our healthy personality, full potential is crucial!

Fearlessness brings with it the conviction that everything in our lives is part of our destiny, exactly what we need in order to become who we really are. Not only is it all right to be myself, it is even all right to let events be themselves. This means entering into a wholehearted engagement with our circumstances rather than arguing with them. Fear argues with circumstances. "No, I do not want that. Do not let that in." Love says: "Let it all happen just as it needs to." In Jung's words, this is "the unconditional yes to that which is, without subjective protest." The givens of existence live through us with our unreserved assent.

Only now does it become clear that to be loving is the same as to be vulnerable. To be vulnerable means to let pain in, not by choice but because it is what is real at the moment. What kind of pain? The ordinary, normal pain that happens in any relationship when people betray you, do things to hurt you, lie to you, leave you, ask too much, or give too little. All of this brings pain. Love means vulnerability—liability—to this. "Yes, I can integrate all of this because it is all human experience that every adult has to have an inlet for."

This is empowering vulnerability to pain, to change, and to loss. The vulnerability of the victim is disempowering: "poor me, kick me, hurt me, deceive me, I want to suffer." Instead, this is the vulnerability described in *The Way of the Tao.* "When we defend ourselves with love we are invincible." See the *paradox: you are invincible when you are vulnerable to what love may bring.* Vulnerable means defended only by that which integrates—handles—all that occurs. The combination in the healthy adult is: defenselessness and resourcefulness.

Consider this little poem by Edwin Markham:

> *They drew a circle to shut me out:*
> *Heretic, rebel, a thing to flout.*
> *But love and I had the wit to win,*
> *We drew a circle and brought them in.*

First, they feared me, so "They drew a circle to shut me out." Then their fear looked for a label: "Heretic, rebel..." They do not integrate, do not let me in. They "flout" me. They push me outside of their circle. But love from me turns it around, an unconditional responsiveness of love toward those who hate, i.e., refuse to integrate, me. The Sermon on the Mount proposes: "Bless those who persecute you. Be kind

to those who hurt you. Pray for those who calumniate you."
Integrate it all. Let it all in. Integrate those who alienate you.

LOVE AND ABUSE

Within a relationship, a partner who fears love may
become abusive toward you, either emotionally or physically.
You endure it, maybe because of your own fear of abandonment or because you are so hooked to that person (addic-
tively) that you seem unable to go. "It is unacceptable but I
still go along with it."

Look back at your life experience, and ask yourself,
"Who taught me to endure this?" Those are your afflicting
forces along your journey to wholeness. They taught you that
you had no right to happiness. "Who helped me refuse this?"
Those are your assisting forces, your angels and guides, who
taught you that happiness was a legitimate option.

When you do the work of confronting the fear, your
statement may change to: "It is unacceptable and I'm doing
something about it." How differently that statement will res-
onate in your psyche! Your body says "hooray," feels healthier, and joins you in the fight. When your body hears "It's
unacceptable and I am still going along with it," you crumple
up, defenseless and without resource.

Does unconditional love mean letting ourselves be
abused? No, our love is unconditional but our choices are
conditioned by our adult boundaries. I love you unconditionally but I cannot live with you because you are an alcoholic
refusing help, or a batterer refusing to change. Perhaps I keep
thinking of better ways to cope rather than newer ways to
equip myself to face my fears. I fear leaving this relationship
which is loveless, purposeless, empty, abusive and unwork-
able. I fear leaving because then I might be lonely. This fear is
a signal that tells me to equip myself to handle loneliness. Or
I can—ironically—simply run from the whole thing by staying in the abusive relationship. I fear either the prospect of

equipping myself for life alone or the pain of life alone. The former is appropriate fear, because I fear hard work that will be new to me. To be defeated by the prospect of loneliness is to be defeated by something unreal, what Jung calls neurotic fear. In this example is also the belief that I do not have a right to happiness, so why do what it takes to find it?

When we say love integrates all that is, we do not mean allowing abuse. What is the distinction between letting anything in and being taken over by something? A healthy person lets in that which honors her boundaries, as opposed to: "I let people do anything they want to me." Allowing people to use you as a doormat does not coincide with the integrating power of love. It is the victim's vulnerability as opposed to healthy vulnerability which allows normal, occasional pain to occur but does not put up with it permanently. "If your remaining detached only encourages unjust aggression, take a strong stand...with no ill-intent," says the Dalai Lama.

Fear's way can be becoming aloof to the pain in intimate human relating. I dodge it before it ever gets to me. Men often react to oncoming pain with an immediate recourse to reason and logic. Women sometimes take flight into tears or the victim role. But whatever role you choose, based on your background and training, you are defending yourself against the full onslaught of your circumstances. How can you deal with it if you have not allowed yourself to feel it? We have to *feel* before we can *deal*.

When a relationship is going well, you might do something to mess it up. "I am not used to this because in my childhood there was so much stress and distress, I imagined that is what life is always supposed to be like." The something inside that tells you to create an uproar may be a fear of the ongoing, consistent, serene love. Very few of us want to "lie down in green pastures...beside the still waters...where our soul is restored."

In the Hero's Journey story, the hero leaves a familiar or comfortable home and crosses over the threshold into a land of struggles where there are bold new tasks to face. Look at the task that Dorothy faced when she went to Oz: to seize the broomstick from the witch. That is a much more enormous task than the one she had at home which was only to take care of a dog. When she crossed the threshold over to this other world, she met the shadow, both positive and negative. The negative shadow is personified by the wicked witch who is full of greed and hate. The positive shadow is personified by the good witch who shows love and courage. If Dorothy had been scared off by that first appearance of the wicked witch so that she woke up from the dream, she would have been back where she started. No journey to newer consciousness or greater power would have been possible. *Is this why we wake up from a frightening dream sometimes? Is it because we are not ready to embark on a journey to new consciousness? Do we awake from the struggle because we cannot integrate what was happening in the dark Oz inside us?* Our fear protects us in that instance. However, when we find ourselves, as Dorothy did, at the threshold of an adventure, and see the terrifying witch, if we say, "I see you and am willing to do battle with you," then we are strong enough to go into the world of the new struggle. Our fear protects us from what we are not ready to handle and our fearlessness equips us to handle it.

Fear is thus the threshold guardian that protects you from entering a place that holds dangers too terrible for your current level of strength. Appropriate fear is like that threshold guardian. If the fear is so great that you cannot deal with it, you have to pull back and build your strength first. You say with the Zen master, "This being the case, how can I proceed?" Our fears point to where our work lies.

If less fear means more love, where does this love come from? All fears have been learned. There are a few that are inborn such as the fear of loud noises and the fear of being dropped. But we were not born with the fear of commitment. That fear was conditioned into us. Where does the love come from if the fear comes from conditioning? The love must come from unconditionality. The unconditionality inside us is our true self, the God archetype within. This is our basic aliveness, the liveliness that makes us want to face what faces us! When fear sits on aliveness we hold an unintegrated excitement. The aliveness is the cathedral and the fear is the gargoyle sitting on it and seemingly holding it down. Love bursts out of aliveness, fear suppresses the aliveness. Maslow said: "The voice of the divine in us is counterpoised not by the voice of the devil but by the voice of fear."

> *Courage means heart.*
> *Courage is how love lets in*
> *What fear rules out.*

WHEN LOVE WALKS IN?

Unconditional love is the very best builder of the immune system. The natural instinct of the body is to want to take love in and to experience the joy and harmony that comes from it. If someone does not let it in, he is having to put out effort to interrupt an instinct toward health and happiness.

But love also comes at you as a will and an intention focused on you with an unconditional desire for you and an unconditional affirmation of your loveability. In other words, it is just what you always wanted but it has a force that can be taxing. You need the capacity to receive it safely. This happens when we are loved safely and securely in early life. This is the mirroring we have referred to earlier in this book and now can define more fully: unconditional positive regard for your feelings and freedom by attention, affection, acceptance, and allowing. Mirroring by a parent equips you to receive love from another adult. If that mirroring did not happen, then you may fear love and have to *learn* how to receive it in adult life.

Love can scare us because we are required to be vulnerable in order to let it into our lives. Vulnerability has become associated with the frightening prospect of abandonment, an isolation from which there might be no returning. This may be the core fear of our unique life story, and all our inhibitions, defenses, flights, and mistakes in relationships may hearken back to this one psychological ancestor. This fear hurts and interrupts us because it was never mirrored. No one ever gave us permission to feel such a fear safely. Instead, it was associated with shame and inadequacy. Our work is to mirror that fear in ourselves, to grant it hospitality by showing it attention, acceptance, and affection and allowing it to have its full career. Then and only then does it comfortably breathe its last. (A clue to our core fear is this: It will be the reverse of how we first felt truly loved. If we felt loved when some one *stayed* with us, then our fear is usually of the opposite: someone going away, i.e., abandoning us.)

When we run from love, we are inviting F.E.A.R. to last: Fleeing the Experience of Authentic Reality. The alternative is to let others love us in their awkward but touching ways. Such defenselessness in us shifts us into resourcefulness! We begin to ask for the love we want. We can then face love's challenges with a coherent sense of ourselves and a trust that letting love in will not fragment us but enrich our wholeness. When we risk being loved by others and tell them how it works best for us, we become nurturant to ourselves, and this is the best way to build trust in ourselves.

There are other reasons love may be scary. Since it wants nothing from you, it gives you no excuse to play your game of: "I'm afraid I might lose something if I allow this." It keeps giving, so you have to be the one to reject it. "I will keep on loving you; you have to be the one to stop it." It nourishes as it comes toward you, so it takes away your complaint about being deprived. Now I can no longer play the game of "poor me." Love is filling me; it is nourishing me. I have no excuses left; love takes them all away. I have to adopt an abundance rather than a deficiency model.

Love has an authentic feeling in it so you are challenged to follow suit and become authentic in the face of it by feeling something in response to it. It has power and it confers power, so you have to give up the victim game. It speaks to you with an engaged focus so you finally have the attention that you always wanted. It declares that you are good enough as you are and there is no chance left to hide in low self-esteem. It imposes only one obligation and that is: "be real." *Is this why it is so terrifying?*

Romance automatically suspends the fear of love and postpones the fear of closeness. It comes up during the next phase: conflict. It is only when you struggle with your partner and no longer see him as an ego ideal that fear arises. The loss of the ego ideal means grief and that may be the foundation of our fear. After the romance, she no longer has you on a pedestal, but comes at you with the will and intention of unconditional authenticity. The real has displaced the ideal. Only when that happens does the mechanism of suspension of the fear of love cease to be operable. Or another way of saying it is, "The closer you get to commitment to a real person, the more will you feel the fear of love."

How do I tell if I have this fear of love? Are there some signals that I could look for in relationships? How do I know if I am living behind the wall? A person who is afraid of love is one who wants to be in control. Wanting to be in control is another way of saying: I am afraid of having to grieve. I am afraid that if you do not give me what I want I will feel bad and I will have to grieve the loss. *I do not really control to get my way as much as to avoid how bad I will feel if I do not get my way.*

Another signal of the fear of love is unresolved, ongoing anger, an undertow of resentment in a relationship. In childhood, you may have had to fight with your mother or father in order to take care of yourself, to protect your own boundaries. Now you may find it hard to experience adult closeness without believing that you still have to fight in order to be safe. And where would you do this except in your primary relationship? What we had to do before, every cell of our body believes we still have to do. We enter relationships still on guard from childhood, still tilting at windmills.

Somebody who refuses to fight may be afraid of that feeling in himself and the possible reaction in you toward him: rejection. "I refuse to argue since it is childish. You do not listen to what I say anyway. It is not going to make any difference. I said what I had to say and you do not believe it so let's not even discuss it." The person who rationalizes like this could also be one who pouts or gives you the silent treatment or withholds sex. The person who says, "I'm not going to fight with you; you're stupid," may be hierarchically fixated. "I am above fighting," is the same as "I am above you." "I am above you" is the same as "I do not want to be equal to you; I do not want to be close to you; I fear being loved by you; I fear love."

Resolved fighting leads to making up and the experience of more intimacy than before. I may fear that eventuality. I do not want to arrive at the point where real intimacy might happen, or real respect, or real equality. We know that if we fight we bond and become more intimate. All mammals fight. As equals, siblings fight. When mammals fight with each other, they learn how to coordinate their body movements; they learn how to play without drawing blood; they learn how to grow in power and how to respect the power of others.

In Greek mythology, Harmony is the daughter of Aphrodite and Ares, Love and War. Intimate harmony results from the fighting between two people who love each other. A healthy relationship is one in which there is occasional fighting, frequent resolution, and ever-increasing bonding.

Finally, a strong signal of the fear of love is holding back from relating and commitment because of the fear of rejection. What happens when you are rejected? You experience loss and grief. Could the fear of rejection be, in large part, the fear of grief? Rejection is a condition of existence; it happens to everyone. Part of our inner strength, our basic liveliness, is to feel a sense of loss and to feel grief about loss. To say "I can't relate because I fear rejection" is saying "I fear my own feelings." I fear the grief I might feel when rejection happens. "I am afraid that you will remind me of how unlovable I have always believed myself to be, and I do not ever want to face that. I am afraid you will make me grow up."

The other side of this coin is to see that we are afraid of acceptance too! If I am accepted, I have to be intimate; if I am rejected, I have to work through the grief of loss. If I am accepted by you, then it really is possible to be loved and I am not unlovable. I will be left with no excuse for avoiding commitment. If I am rejected, I will grieve in the present, and if I am accepted, I will grieve about the past. Most people who fear rejection fear acceptance just as much, and deny it vociferously!

Also, if I am lovable to you and I was not lovable to my parents, then I bring to an end the belief that nobody really loves anybody, and I have to admit my parents may not have loved me. I can feel in the way I am being loved now that this is what love is really like. I can feel that *this is authentic and this does not match what I received from them.* Your love makes me a mourner and an orphan—though it mirrors me too!

LOVING SOMEONE WHO IS AFRAID

When you ask someone who is afraid of your love to let you get close, what you are really asking him to do is "die of fright." Being aware of that brings some compassion into how you approach someone afraid of your love.

It also helps to remember not to pursue, because when you pursue, all you will have is someone who is caught. What is the feeling of an animal with one foot stuck in your trap? Angry, afraid, and desperate. That is what you may provoke when you pursue.

What can you do? You can try every charm you know. You try everything you can, and then if it does not work, you let go of it. This is the Western way: to expend the effort, to try every trick we know, to proclaim and show our feelings. In medieval times, it was thought that lion cubs were born deaf and the father lion's roar woke them up. He roars, in order to wake the young lions out of their sleep. When you express your feelings, you produce a lion's roar that awakens the unconscious person so he can hear the words: "I love you and you do not have to be afraid."

From an Eastern perspective, from a more meditative standpoint, *you just stand there with your arms outstretched and with a look of welcome.* Or you can just sit on the wall and be a witness of something that has nothing to do with you. You simply watch; and that person will see that you are paying attention, from a safe distance for him. For you, it is breaking the habit of taking everything personally, or trying to fix it, or trying to change it, or coming to the rescue, or trying to solve it. When you give up the belief that you have that kind of power over other people, you look so harmless, so tender, so disarming. When the person behind the wall looks up at you sitting there, he may not be so afraid because for once somebody is not coming at him with the attempt to control, crowd, or change him. You are letting someone be scared, no matter how much it hurts you to see it, no matter how sure you are that you have the answer to his problem. That is the mirroring that may heal and open someone.

There is a poem by Emily Dickinson which says, "You there, I here, with just the door ajar—that oceans are." A small but vast space occurs between two people. It occurs when you are not trying to fix or control. It is as wide as the ocean but it is also as narrow as a door ajar. It takes enormous courage to allow that space to open up, that gap to open up between you and someone else. I do not have to rush in and grab you. I do not have to shake you or release you. I can simply be here and let it be all right that you are there. We both can feel the freedom and the spaciousness. Paradoxically, this is the very gesture that can build intimacy from respectful presence.

The affirmation that may fit here is: "I give up control and let the chips fall where they may." When I do that, I honor reality rather than impose my paradigm upon it. This is another paradox: as I let go of control, I am truly empowered, because I finally become harmonious with the nature of things instead of being at odds with it. Reality and I are allies. I am no longer using my mind to dictate how things are supposed to be. Instead, I trust that the way things unravel—with me sitting there on the wall watching in the loving, nonintrusive way—will ultimately be just exactly what is best for me and the other. Real love's greatest feat is to accept the other's reality without the need to impose my own.

Emerson wrote in his *Essay on Nature:* "I was walking through the woods and I noticed that the green things were nodding to me; they were affirming me; they were, in effect, saying yes, we appreciate you and you appreciate us." This is a sense of harmony with the way it is, rather than how I make it. Now we have the ability to trust the gap that opens up between us people. It will close when the timing is just right for everyone.

You are with somebody who lives behind the wall, a high wall. How do you know when to roar or when to sit and observe? Your intuition will tell you. You will have enough of a sense of the other person to realize what might have an impact. When you are truly sitting on the wall as a witness, or when you are truly standing with your arms out-stretched, welcoming, then the other person sees the harmless, authentic, loving feeling in you. The roaring is a method, and the "just sitting" is a happening. Either can work.

FEAR OF SELF-DISCLOSURE

Fear can make it impossible to feel all our feelings.
The person we describe as shut down, cold, distant,
  may really be afraid.
His fear is a blockade against all his other feelings.

Compassion may help show him
what is waiting inside for release.

The fear of letting other people know what you are feeling, or who you really are, is ultimately a fear of self-acceptance and of the risk of finding acceptance—being loved—by others. Imagine what contempt must have been shown to us in early life to make us afraid to give the only gift that we really can give, which is the gift of our true self. What danger made it necessary to don disguises, so that the simple reality of who we are would not appear? A person who remains always the same, who stays in character, may be somebody who maintains this fear. "Out of character" means taking a chance on opening more of oneself. To ex-pose is to explore. In this context, you might also feel a fear of free speech. You cannot really say what you want to say. You have to keep custody over your words. "Do my words uphold an image and insure the safety of the character I want to present, or do they throw my image to the wind and expose me authentically?" Naked really means, after all, divested of ego, the part of us that fears the real. What self-defeat! We may be afraid to show the very parts of ourselves that make us lovable, e.g., our vulnerability.

The real being, with no status, is always going in and out
through the doors of your face.   —Lin Chi

THE SEXUAL CONNECTION

Another signal of the fear of love might be in sexualizing any authentic affection. You cannot hug somebody, or be hugged, without feeling sexually aroused. People who react that way may be afraid of love—as opposed to highly sexed! In the heat of sexual passion, you do not really have to look at the other person. You do not really have to talk to the other person, except for a few grunts and four-letter words. Intimacies may mask the fear of intimacy!

Some people are very uncomfortable about cuddling. Some see cuddling only as foreplay to sex. Every gesture is aimed somehow toward the bedroom. He may say, "I have a very high level of testosterone." But he may also have a very high level of panic about the possibility of being close!

"Sex is really only touch, the closest of all touch. And it's touch we're afraid of. We're only half-conscious and half-alive," wrote D.H. Lawrence. It is normal that most of us associate fear with sex. Besides the fact that we equate sex with performance, ego, and conquering, we have also inherited fear-creating beliefs about it. Our earliest experience of sex may have been punitive, prohibitive, or repressive. The result may be that fear lies deep in the soul of my sexual self. There is something inherently wrong and dangerous with sexual pleasure derived from my own body or even from the body of another. All I can do is admit that sad inheritance and over-ride it. It may never vanish totally but it does not have to stop me.

At the same time, people who have a fear of closeness figured out long ago that intense sex can certainly make it unnecessary to be truly intimate. When intimacy becomes so strong that more of a commitment is demanded, or I have to invest more of myself in the relationship, I might become terrified. I might display a sexual problem or lack of interest or might even start an affair with somebody else. When the sex begins to become a way of *bonding,* or a way of deepening the commitment, when it changes from romantic athletics into a mature exchange and real closeness, it may become threatening.

Sex includes removing our clothes, the dream symbol of dropping our Persona, the mask we present to the world for its approval. Intimate sex is stripping for a skin search. *Can I withstand that thorough an inquiry into myself?*

The intense sex of the romance stage is fueled by a deep

self-disclosure. Sex may become flat or dull later because self-disclosure has become too threatening. We then de-juice our sexuality. Our fear of self-disclosure may be behind our "loss of sexual interest." Intimacy may require more from us than we are willing to give. Sex may be fun going in and then demanding and scary to continue. We are seduced and then we withhold because the cost keeps escalating.

Sex is the gateway, after all, to some difficult conditions of existence: I may be rejected; I may not be loved as I had hoped; I may have to love or give or be authentic. I may be seen or seen through. My shadow side may show through despite my vigilant attempts to mask it with my winsome facade. All this may terrify me! I may appear in all the rags of my emotional poverty, vulnerability, and downright mean-ness: the very things I hoped to hide by getting you to love me! The human comedy: here I am hiding what I most need to reveal to be authentic and authentically loved!

Full sexual potential happens in the context of rigorous emotional honesty and spiritual adulthood. Good sex is not about technique or charm or even appeal. It is about trans-parency. A full range of sexual function means full range of human emotion, not full range of genital motion! New tech-niques, new underwear, and new toys cannot quell the under-lying fear of self-revelation and self-giving—especially with no guarantee of being accepted!

When I am sure of myself and have a self-concept that is sturdy and separate from yours (though available for related-ness to yours) then I can face the challenges of a sexual rela-tionship. These challenges are the conditions of existence, the givens of relating: I may give myself and not receive; I may show myself and not be approved; I may not be happy all the time. In other words, love will not exempt me from adult-hood.

If I lack a strong sense of self, I may instead operate as a false self, hoping that someone will fall for my elaborate, long-standing camouflage. Some couples are secretly terrified to take the chance that either partner will see what is behind the veil. They coddle each other's egos to forestall the fall of the veil and the exposé of the vacancy behind it. *Is this the implicit bargain that you and I have called commitment? Have we used sex to maintain our fear of closeness?*

Sex cannot create intimacy. We bring intimacy to sex when we let go of our fear of giving or receiving, of knowing and being known, of letting the chips fall where they may and picking them up when they do. Intimacy is found by letting go of control and saying Yes to such conditions of relating, with all their ups and downs. One of these conditions is that sex contains anxiety naturally because it confronts us with the risk of self-disclosure. To accept anxiety makes more sense than to attempt to relax it away. It is riding in the direction the horse is going.

If I can go with this process, my relationship becomes not a cauldron in which my shadow can be submerged but a crucible from which my true self can emerge. In other words, I became my true self when I let someone I love see me and my fears. Revelation strengthens and articulates the adult self. Such gutsy, ruthless self-disclosure and self-giving increases sexual desire and desirability faster than any acrobatics, aromatics, or romantics.

Authentic sex appeal thrives on the intimate sharing of our scared selves. This happens best when we have stood alone long enough to find out who we are and be happy with the findings. The prerequisite of intimacy is personal differentiation. We are not one; we are two in one bond. The bond of adult intimacy does not dissolve our individuality. We can use this bond to store anger, to stave off fear, or to shore up love. Healthy partners are standing hand-in-hand and yet alone.

This happens to people who have faced their fears of aloneness and abandonment, accepting them both as ingredients—givens—of any human life. It means letting go of Dorothy's wish for a Wizard, Pinocchio's wish for a land of ice cream, or Cinderella's wish for a rescuing prince. It means letting go of the belief that anyone has to love us unconditionally, or be there for us consistently, or satisfy us fully. (Those are only the inner child's three wishes to the parent-genie in the, alas, sealed bottle.)

No relationship can save us from the fear of abandonment. Anyone who matters may leave us. An adult knows that a relationship grants no such exemptions. The healthy adult is not looking for a relationship that protects him/her from the possibility of abandonment. He/she has a program to handle such an event: grieving and grieving more. The deeper the intimate bond, the more keenly will losses be felt. No relationship shields us from grief or creates a safe harbor from pain. Such contingencies will always appear possible on the horizon to those willing to look.

Paradoxically, when the illusion of fusion is gone, we find ourselves dancing on a broader stage: that of the universe. Our oneness with nature and with all humans becomes clear, perhaps for the first time.

Finally, beneath the fear of love is the desire for it. Beneath the desire for sex is the craving for love. This can make us *sexualize our need for nurturance*. We look for sex when we really desire loving closeness. Once we recognize the mistaken direction, we can find the path where love comes first and sex is the act of its joy at being found.

> *The essence of this archetypal homeland toward which the psychotherapeutic partners travel is the realization of the subjective sovereignty of each human being....Being truly awake is a place of power from which we may have true governance of our lives.* —J. Bugental

THE FEAR OF GIVING/RECEIVING

Intimacy means giving and receiving within a committed bond of love. What is given and received is love, truth, feeling, and closeness, both emotional and physical. The fear of giving and receiving refers to intimacy in relationships, but it also could refer to distress about money: spending it, saving it, lending it, returning it, giving it, receiving it, earning it, etc. Anybody who has an issue with one of these definitely will have problems with intimacy because intimacy is about freedom in giving and receiving, and money is the symbol of that exchange.

FEARS OF ABANDONMENT AND ENGULFMENT

Two familiar fears arise in the context of intimacy. The fear of giving is the same as the fear of commitment and of showing love. The fear of receiving is the fear of being loved, which, as we saw above, can be even more terrifying. The fear of giving and receiving may be the fear of engulfment. The fear of comings and goings may be the fear of abandonment. The fear of engulfment is the fear of someone getting too close, and the fear of abandonment is the fear that someone will go away and we will not survive it. ("Not to survive" we can now define as being defenseless and resourceless.) A healthy person is one who can relate to someone without being overwhelmed by the fear of abandonment if the other goes away and without being overwhelmed by the fear of engulfment if the other draws too near.

The fear of abandonment and the fear of engulfment are the most puissant fears in intimacy. They represent our deepest doubts about our own worthiness to be loved. Others cannot love me permanently and loyally. They will leave me once they really know me or tire of me. This is the fear of abandonment. The fear of engulfment also has to do with self-diminishment: I have so little within me that if I let someone really touch me at a soulful level, I will lose something of myself. As the poem *The Hound of Heaven* says: "Lest having him, I must have naught beside!"

The fear of abandonment and the fear of engulfment are

often visible in a relationship in which one partner is afraid primarily of abandonment and the other of engulfment. She is afraid he will leave and so she clings; he fears she is getting too close and so he flees. This keeps them in an endless dance in which one chases and the other runs. One partner is needy and desperate and the other is aloof and harried. A neurotic fit has occurred, and the partners may continue this pattern for years. Ironically, it is often the partner with the fear of abandonment that leaves! She is so afraid of being alone that she may line up a back-up partner, and when that new partner seems to offer all that she could possibly want, she may leave the original partner for him.

Abandonment is the central fear in childhood. Our parents are vitally necessary for our survival, and we associate the loss of them with annihilation. This may happen physically or by the loss of their emotional engagement to us. At the same time, our instinctive drive toward freedom makes us push them away if they hold on to us too tightly. The sense of being smothered or owned and not being able to defend ourselves may lead to a fear of engulfment.

The fears of abandonment and of engulfment may carry over into adult relationships. All through life, separation anxiety may make us cling to or placate a partner to hold onto him or her. Such behavior is really fear of abandonment, though it may look like love. We may feel we need more and more distance in a relationship, not wanting to be too committed to someone lest we lose our liberty. This may be the fear of engulfment, though it looks like bravado and self-reliance. Imagining the pain it must have taken for us to become this way leads to compassion for ourselves and others who feel the same fears.

Both fear of abandonment and fear of engulfment are phantom fears, like phantom pain. Abandonment and engulfment already happened in the powerless past of childhood and cannot really happen to adults. An adult cannot be abandoned, only left, not engulfed, only crowded.

Early fear was felt cellularly and was indeed real. Defensive postures were necessary, but defenses generalize cellularly in adulthood and do not expire. It takes conscious work to undo them. Ironically, as long as we keep using defenses, we actually maintain the original force of the fear.

Everyone feels abandoned at times and engulfed at times. These are conditions of relational existence. Adults have a reasonable program to handle them: "When you go, I grieve and let you go." "When you get too close, I ask you to give me more room!"

In abandonment:

We fear abandonment rightly since it means the loss of mirroring, and that is necessary for the survival of our very identity. We also fear the grief we will feel when someone leaves. The fear of abandonment may be the fear of grief.

We abandon ourselves at times, e.g., abandoning our body or our integrity or our boundaries to hold onto someone. We may abdicate some part of ourselves when we cling to another for dear life. Freedom from this fear means restoring the disenfranchised psychic territories of ourselves.

Abandonment is terrifying also because we feel so powerless at the moment it occurs. This combination of fear and powerlessness is what made an original abandonment experience from childhood leave so indelible a mark on us.

We feel panic when the other withdraws, so we pursue more intensely, and this makes a partner panic and push us away even more. Our way of taking care of ourselves is precisely what makes us the more abandoned! It is a self-defeat in the guise of self-protection.

The fear of death is also about the fear of abandonment, of the final isolation, of the loss of the bonds that sustain us. Death is so scary because it seems to be an abandonment of our body by our soul.

There is a cruel irony in the fact that the fear of intimacy is directly proportional to the fear of abandonment. The more afraid we are of being abandoned, the more afraid we are of getting close. *Has my tenderness been bottled up with my fears?*

In engulfment:

When we fear engulfment, we may be afraid of letting in attention or intimacy. Focus on us in childhood may have felt like confinement or diminishment when attention meant scrutiny and invasion by overprotective parents. Later, an honest emotional communication may feel like an onslaught or invasion. Engulfment fear may thus be sparked by a partner simply sharing his or her feelings or inquiring about us with solicitude. Somehow these innocent approaches of intimacy recreate terrors of the past, and we automatically reenact our defenses against them.

We may feel that the only way to protect our boundaries is to remain at arm's length. We then feel compelled to push people away for safety's sake. Closeness and commitment may seem like threats against or incursions into the tenuous integrity of our identity.

In the terror of being held too tightly or loved too intensely is an impulse to run that becomes quite subtle in the many forms it may take: coldness, refusals to make commitments, need for more space and more secrets, indifference, intolerance, rigid boundaries, embarrassment about affection in public, etc. We may even confuse a partner by seducing and then withholding our affection.

This fear may also manifest itself as entitlement to be served by the other while not believing one has any obligation to reciprocate. Fear of engulfment often contains an ego inflation as a defense against vulnerability and intimacy.

The partners who fear engulfment are less likely to leave because they have been successful at not being caught! When they themselves are left, they may discover their own abandonment fears for the first time. They become aware of how deeply bereft they are by the loss of their partner and they discover the deep well of neediness and loneliness in themselves. If they can admit these feelings to themselves and to a future partner, they have a real chance for freedom from the fear of engulfment and true intimacy with someone who can respect their vulnerability.

Finally, in fear of abandonment we show fear and repress anger. In fear of engulfment we show anger and repress fear!

TO DO: WORKING WITH THESE FEARS

Everyone feels the fear of abandonment and the fear of engulfment. Our task is not to stop feeling fears but to allow them and not to be stopped by them. We seek the breadth of courage to let the other go without being consumed by a fear of abandonment and to let the other draw near without being panicked by the fear of engulfment.

Here is a program that may help:

- Admit your fears to yourself and to your partner.

- Allow yourself to feel your fears fully, cradling them acceptingly.

- Act as if your fears were not obstacles to closeness or safety: If you fear engulfment, draw an inch closer than you can stand for one minute more than you can stand. If you fear abandonment, let the other go an inch farther away than you can stand for a minute longer than you can stand. Repeat this over and over, adding more time and more space on each occasion.

- Bust yourself on despair:

   This is how I am/or how he or she is.

   This is how I always was/or how he or she always was.

This is how all my family is/or how he or she is.

• Say this to your partner: I may not shield you from the fear of abandonment, or engulfment, and I do not ask you to shield me. I accept such fears as conditions of human existence, as givens of relating. I choose to acknowledge fear of abandonment or of engulfment and work through it. I go on living rather than evading my fear and thereby go on fearing.

FEAR OF OTHERS' FEELINGS

You may believe you have to walk on eggshells around certain people. You do not look forward to seeing them. You are probably afraid of them but you have never called it fear. An adult refuses to settle for being afraid of anybody. To keep spending time with someone who threatens you, without trying to change it, is abusing your scared child inside. You are saying "I'll put you into the bull ring where I know you will be bruised." To wake up every morning beside someone you fear is the heaviest of all molestations of your inner child. This willingness is insidious psychically because it means you are willing to threaten your own most vulnerable self.

What is happening when someone scares us? Here are three possibilities:

This person may intimidate you because *he* is afraid. You are feeling the ricochet of his fear. For instance, he may fear closeness and he might be using his intimidating manner to keep you at a distance. So he acts in a way that makes you scared of him. He has learned over the years: "If I scare people with my brusque manner or pugnacity they will not get close."

Secondly, it could be that you are experiencing early childhood fears somehow triggered by this person. This might be the case especially when you believe you cannot even defend yourself. This may be a tip-off to a childhood scenario of powerlessness, now reappearing. Heidegger said: "The dreadful has already happened." The dreadful thing happened long ago and now we see a recurrence of it, a replica of it, in the face of someone in the adult world. The same childhood terrors come up from our body, cellularly, in response to an old memory. We are suddenly feeling again as defenseless as we once were.

The third possibility is that you are meeting up with the shadow, the darker side of the other. You might even be seeing the shadow of yourself in the other person. As mentioned above, the shadow is the unconscious side of yourself that you do not want to see. If you feel admiration toward a person that you fear, you may be projecting your own positive shadow, your own unacknowledged potential. You wish for what you already have. If you feel dread, with a wish for vengeance toward someone, it may be a sign of the negative shadow coming into play. You despise in someone else what is denied in yourself.

What about the fear of a person's feelings that are or might be directed at you? It is unlikely that anyone fears true feelings because true feelings are a form of attention. Somebody is focusing in an engaged and noninvasive way on you. It is a fulfillment of one of your basic needs.

We have so rarely had this kind of attention paid to us! If someone were to direct a true, authentic, unintimidating, non-violent feeling toward us, we would welcome it! If it is a real feeling, it will garner our attention immediately and will initiate a true adult exchange. We will stop in our tracks and be rapt in attention because feeling comes from attention to attention.

But most of us do not see real feelings. Instead, we see the layers of drama that surround a feeling, i.e., the layers of ego: fear, attachment, control, judgment, entitlement. These are all forms of violation that are meant to engender fear. Someone is angry at you. What if, instead of feeling his pure anger come through to you (which is what it seems to look like), you are sensing judgment: "You're to blame," "I expect you to change." The angry person is playing out a theatrical version of anger which is really a combination of judgment, expectation, blame, threat, guilt-tripping, etc. In drama, a scared ego is seeking a scared child.

Is anger a way of expressing love? It is. Love includes all the feelings, but it does not include any of the judgments or the dramatic layers that cover up the feelings. Deep down, there is a soft center in every feeling, but we do not always find it. A golf ball is hard, but in the center of it is something soft and totally harmless. That is what feeling is like. It always has a harmless, soft center that can be found if we look deeply enough. *Will I make the time?*

If you become caught up in the expectation, the judgment, the blame, etc.—the sports of ego—then you are distracted from the real feeling and so no true communication occurs. A couple may say, "Yes, we communicate; we are always expressing our feelings." That may not be true. It could be that all they are expressing is blame, expectation, judgment, threats, etc. None of that is feeling. There is no real communication unless you are expressing the actual feeling behind it all. Such real feelings are nonviolent, nonintrusive, non-invasive.

Why would we be scared by the ego layers of drama? Because they say loudly and clearly: you have to change, you are bad, you are wrong, you cannot fix this for me, you are worthless. These may be reminiscent of abusive messages you heard in childhood, making such drama doubly powerful in its effect upon you. It can devastate your personal power and your self-esteem. Each one of the dramatic layers is a verdict that triggers some old message: I am still at the mercy of others; I still can let other people get to me this way. I am feeling attacked and am out-of-control, utterly defenseless.

I appear to be afraid of being powerless when I am really afraid of being powerful. I fear having the power to stand up to someone, to cut through all the layers, and to direct myself to the person, saying, "You can't do that to me; I don't allow that." Instead, I tread softly and think I fear feelings when really *I fear the theatrical disguises being used by someone as scared as I.*

Some people are not only scared but also have malice toward you. They may be *deliberately* trying to scare or hurt you. They may call it: "teaching you a lesson," i.e., punishing you. This is hate—strong anger with an unforgiving desire for vengeance. Malice is a form of violence and such a mean streak may never go away. In a relationship, beware of thinking, "I can change him, I can soften him up." It takes more than kindness or even therapy; it takes a spiritual awakening, a conversion—and it may never happen.

Some partners or parents are neurotically anxious. You might have had a parent who became very irritable and spanked you, but underneath you knew there was love. But some parents, or partners, are mean and malicious and underneath is a deep disturbance which you cannot fix and they cannot fix either. And from those people you can only run.

TO DO: MINDFULNESS

If you were to sit mindfully—contemplatively as a fair witness of life's conditions—with one of your own feelings, you might peel away each of its ego layers: blame, expectations, judgments, the need to fix it, guilt, threats, etc. This mindfulness is the best path to freedom from drama.

"My partner betrayed me, became involved with someone else, and ran away with her. He has abandoned, humiliated, and rejected me." These are the layers of drama that cover the true feeling of grief. "Abandoned, humiliated and rejected" are judgments and interpretations. "She is gone and I am grieving" is the pure expression of my feeling. The dramatic (and much more interesting) way to put it is, "I am abandoned, I am humiliated, I am rejected, he betrayed me, she did not keep her agreement, she is no good, etc." Those are all the ego masks that are meant to hide the central feeling which, of course, is very painful to live through. If I can keep telling the story of how I was hurt, abandoned, humiliated, etc., I may never have to feel the grief, and I can keep her wrong and everybody can agree with me that she is wrong. I am comforted by this support. (But real friends will support my grief, not my judgments. They support the real me, not my flight from me.)

What is the central, core feeling and how can I express it simply? I simply sit with my own reality, purely, just as a headline, without any adrenalizing or analyzing or editorializing. This is the mindfulness of "calm abiding" (Shamatha: Tibetan form of meditation). We keep coming back to the conditions of existence: I am alone in my suffering; I cannot rope somebody else into it by blaming, etc. This is spiritual freedom: Buddha's liberation from fear and desire: the legitimate *equilibrium* of pain and joy in a human life. The goal was never to escape fear totally but to find a place for it and a way through it.

Pure feeling makes you powerfully vulnerable. You are showing your softness and the ego does not want to do that. It wants to present the hard surface so it comes up with all the layers that are meant to protect the softness, that is, to hide the vulnerability. Actually you are then hiding the most beautiful thing about yourself which is your ability to express a feeling in a tender, non-violent way.

The ego sets up sentinels around the prisoner inside— the prisoner in this case is the true feeling. You are keeping the true feeling in prison by getting caught up in all the ego's ways of defending its image. It is the fear of self-disclosure and, ultimately, of love. If you take the risk of opening, people would run toward you with open arms because they would feel the disarming attention that was coming to them as you expressed it, and they would love you for it. *Is this what we ultimately fear more than anything?*

Negative excitement is the stress that may surround your daily story line, usually fueled by unfinished emotional business. It is a forgery of your lively energy. Drama means that the things happening to you assume melodramatic proportions: You cannot talk about what is going on in a normal tone of voice. Everything is filled with high-pitched apprehension.

This negative excitement is pain that has fear in it. It contains both elements of a drama: fear and desire. In the real expression of a feeling, you express the feeling and then resolve it. A true feeling is one that ends in resolution. A feeling that is interrupted or protracted and not resolved is drama. If you are used to being sustained in life by drama, you avoid the real expression of feelings.

Since drama means no resolution, it could look to you like a sense of purpose. "I am somebody. I have a purpose because I have so much going on." If this were fulfilled and resolved, I might feel purposeless. If I do not continually have something churning, and I am not continually upset by something, or depressed, then I do not have a sense of purpose. This is addiction! Actually what you are feeling is withdrawal pain when you no longer have a drama on stage. This withdrawal pain makes you create another scene and the cycle continues.

The way to tell that it is a drama is, one, it is not resolved, and, two, it is impossible to be simply a witness of it. You are so caught up in it that you cannot step back and see it for what it is. You are enmeshed in it. You are not relating to it; you are possessed by it. Your story has eaten you up and you are so caught up in the little details of what is going on that there is no "you" left. You cannot do any work on yourself, you cannot handle things because to handle something means to step aside and relate to it. For instance, I find out my partner is involved with someone. I am jealous. (Jealousy is the ego's word for grief: sadness, anger, and fear.) I am over-whelmed with grief which I do not want to express fully and resolve. I want to dump on the other person, tell all my friends what a terrible person she is, etc. I am obsessed with the story. I cannot relate to it because I have become it. It can-not move—emotion means to move out of. This is how it is the opposite of true feeling, i.e., lively energy.

To the outside world, the drama might look very lively because you are running around telling your story, gossiping on the phone, finding out more about what is going on. It looks lively but it is not because lively means moving from feeling to resolution. This is stuck between feeling and reso-lution.

Here is the difference between a soap opera and a great drama: in a soap opera, things are continually happening but there is no processing of the happenings. In a drama, there is contemplation of the meanings and impacts of events throughout the story, e.g., the soliloquies of Shakespeare in which the character steps back from the events and considers them thoughtfully. This is the mindful pause that leads to the healing letting go.

CAN YOU LOVE SOMEONE THAT YOU CONTROL?

Love is not a feeling but a choice, a commitment to mir-ror someone.

It happens originally from a parent to a child.

Mirroring means unconditional, positive regard.

It is shown in four major ways: attention, acceptance, affection, and allowing the other freedom to be and become who he/she is.

These same four elements of love are also our major needs in adult relationships!

To seek the fulfillment of these needs is to ask someone to mirror us as we are.

Freedom is the ability and the right to choose.

Control takes over that right and denies that ability.

So when we control someone we are not loving him/her.

We have omitted the allowing and acceptance elements of mirroring.

We fear letting the other be who he/she really is.

To control is to make someone over in our own image, and that self-mirrored image is what we love, not the true other mirrored as he/she is.

Perhaps most of us achieve only loving moments—special times when we dare to show attention, acceptance, affection, and allowing.

Love only happens when we let go of control and the fear behind it.

In spiritual love, we go one step further and mirror to others the higher power of the heart: unconditional and universal love, perennial wisdom, and healing. Control gives way to letting be; knowing what is best for others gives way to respect for their choices; and making-over gives way to genuine curiosity about their surprising uniqueness.

Can I risk that?

To Do: Letting Love In

Our work on our fear follows a simple path:

admit you are afraid,

allow yourself to feel the fear fully,

act as if fear were not getting in your way.

Allow the one who loves you—and whom you want to love but cannot—to draw an inch closer for a minute longer than you can stand. You will see the humor in your fear as the courage to receive love begins to confer lightness. You play with your pain, you laugh at yourself: "With love's light wings did I o'er perch these walls, for stony limits cannot hold love out and what love can do, that dares love attempt." My desire to be loved and to love is stronger than my fear of it. Love does that; it puts you into a position that makes you no longer so careful about limits: stony limits that I have built around myself—my stony limits that no longer hold love out.

This work involves a willingness to be awkward, to be an amateur. To feel the fear and still let yourself be loved is doing the very opposite of what the wall does. The wall protects the fear. Now you leave the fear unprotected, allowing yourself to feel it, thereby acting as if you were not feeling it. The daily moment and the daily inch impacts exponentially as time goes by because you are teaching your body one cell at a time: "You don't have to be so afraid anymore."

Your partner hugs you. You start shivering and scrunching up. You just cannot stand it, and, to get away, you say: "You know I have to get to work, I can't stay right now, I have to leave." To work on that fear, you let yourself stay in the embrace for one more minute than you can stand. It is awkward and feels painful, but in that one minute your body is finding out: "You can stay and still survive." A message of safety has gone through every cell. Next time you add another minute. And before you know it you can hug as long as you want. Repeated acts of love diminish the fear response both in ourselves and in others. When each partner risks doing something one more minute than each can stand, they are standing together, i.e., intimate.

It is easy to hug; it is hard to be hugged. In a real hug, you do not just hug, you stay long enough to feel hugged. When you hug, you are in control of what happens: the tightness, the time, the position. But when you let yourself be hugged, you are letting the other person have some of the control and some of the power, another road to fearlessness.

Henry and Susan

Both Henry and Susan have become experts in running from love. They are continually fighting or looking for reasons to fight. They bicker in such a toxic and often sarcastic way that nothing is ever resolved and both are left feeling hurt and frustrated. They gather resentments toward one another and have never forgiven one another for anything. Deep-down they are scared to death of the serene bonding that may occur if they give up their egos long enough to hear one another and hold one another's fears. The relationship is not a safe container for such holding, a holding that would allow true intimacy to flourish. They have found a neurotic fit, playing the game of distancing in the guise of relating. Relating, for them, ensures that bonding cannot take place. Actually, in this respect, their relationship is a form of pain. They are stuck in a mutually self-defeating scenario.

Any hope of change will happen only in the context that most frightens them: facing and experiencing their fears and then mutually admitting/holding them. Henry and Susan refuse to do this. If they did pursue closeness instead of distance, they might each say this to one another:

"I fear you. I fear being loved by you. I fear giving myself to you."

Then, they would add:

"I risk loving you. I risk being loved by you. I risk giving myself to you."

Replacing the fear word with the risk word starts the program of change. Then the work becomes: addressing, processing, and resolving the issue of fear. This is how people go on to more healthy adult relating.

But Henry and Susan have another agenda: each of them wants to assert his/her ego in such a way that one of them can win. And what will the winner have as a prize? The shambles of a hurtful, mismatched, futureless affiliation in which each of them can blame the other for his/her unhappiness and neither of them can go on to adult intimacy. They have a contract to protect one another from that. It is called deadlock and needs to be taken by storm.

Part Two:

Taking FEAR

by Storm

5.

Facing Fear

We do not fear things as much as we fear the possibility of not being able to handle what will come up because of them: feelings, grief, the requirement of action, the need to let go or go on.

"Be wise as serpents and innocent as doves!"

Our program for dealing with fear is to combine the dove's defenselessness with the serpent's resourcefulness! We are defenseless in the sense that we allow ourselves to feel the fear fully. We are resourceful in that we act in new ways thereafter.

We are defenseless against many stresses and crises but resourceful in that we have a program to handle them:

If I have a car accident, against which I am defenseless, I also have car insurance and a lawyer as resources.

If I experience a loss, I can do griefwork. I am powerless to avoid losses but resourceful since I can grieve and that process helps me to let go of the pain.

If I have an addiction, I have access to a Twelve Step program.

The Sermon on the Mount is the resource program for handling hurt by another. It opposes the automatic ego program of: get back at him!

The program for handling fear is simple: admit fear, allow yourself to feel fear, and then act with fear as if fear is not stopping you. I *install myself in the very fear I flee*. When we are committed to the work, we do not look at fear as a concept but we look at our scared selves and find a gentle and paradoxical way to loosen the grip fear has over us.

When a good person sees a scared child he shows compassion and holds him. We hold our scared inner child when we allow ourselves to feel our fear defenselessly and handle it resourcefully. Fear has to be loved into the light. That is the real nature of the work.

Everyone has the capacity to ride a horse. Not everyone has the ability. To ride a horse correctly requires learning and practicing skills that give one ability. Ability activates capacity. Handling fear is likewise a capacity that can become an ability by learning the skill. Handling does not mean getting through things in a stoic way: "I handled it very well. I kept a stiff upper lip." Handling fear is riding the wind-horse: you activate a program for courage and you open yourself to a power that may come into play to extend and enrich what you are doing. It is the integration of psychological work and spiritual grace. The psyche, like a Swiss army knife, has blades enough for each task that may arise in the human forest. The same organism that has fear in it has resources in it for the handling of fear. Spiritually, resources are signs of assisting forces within and around us.

You are handling things when your response fits the stimulus. The person who is handling something could look as though he is totally out of control. He could be screaming and crying, beating his fist against the wall. He is handling something because he is showing authentic feelings in an intense way.

A terrible loss has occurred and you are in a paroxysm of grief and totally unable to go to work or to live your life normally for a few days, or for a few weeks. You are handling things because you are feeling and acting upon the grief that is appropriate to the original event. Remember the movies from the 1940s in which, just before going on stage, the comic finds out that his mother has just died? "The show must go on," he says and gives the performance anyway. That person is not loyal to himself; he is loyal to his audience. What if the theater manager were instead to announce: "Al Jolson is appropriately grieving and will not be appearing tonight or any night this week; maybe not even next week, because he is handling his grief and we respect him for it?"

Most people fear feelings. Part of being polite is not to show our feelings because it may make others uncomfortable. Most people will interpret normal assertion of anger, for instance, as aggression, and maybe even reject you because you were angry and let it be known. Underneath this rejection of you is, "I am deathly afraid of anger." If you see that, you might say, "I noticed that when I expressed my anger you seemed taken aback. Because I express it that way does not mean I am out of control or that I will hurt you. If only you could be simply a witness of it, and just allow it, you would notice that my anger does not do any harm." *The stronger and healthier you become, the more explanations you have to give.* To express your authentic liveliness scares other people. They want things to stay on an even keel, and that will not happen if you are handling, expressing, your feelings.

I remember in childhood when I would have a friend over for dinner, and if he was not Italian, he only visited once. I would ask what the matter was. "In your house, people yell. I was scared." I did not even notice that was happening! Recently in my life, I realized that I was myself terrified by the outbursts of violence in my childhood home and by my vulnerability to the out-of-control adults around me. What was being indelibly imprinted in my cells about *fear in the context of love?* Even as late as last week, I shuddered while watching a movie in which a father was angry at a son who was standing close to him. "Move back," I heard myself urge him. "If you get that close, you might get hit!" *And that must be the message I bring—unconsciously and automatically—to relationships.* We were learning about intimacy in every childhood scenario and imago. This is why healthy relating will require a knowledge of and a program for handling our fears. We love more freely and effectively when we let go of the fears that have been shadowing us for a lifetime.

When you are brought up to see healthy anger in the context of safety around you, fear does not arise because you have noticed, again and again, that it does not lead to violence. *What was it like in your childhood home when it came to feelings? Were they expressed openly or was everything kept very polite? Politeness is often the opposite of feeling.*

There are two kinds of fear to handle. Since appropriate fear gives information about real danger, to handle it is simple: flee or fight. Fight it if you can fight it, run away from it if you cannot fight it. Ask the help of someone who can fight it with you. That is dealing appropriately with appropriate fear.

How do we deal with neurotic fear? You fear closeness, abandonment, rejection, success, failure, what other people might think of you. These things do not really hurt you. It is FALSE EVIDENCE APPEARING REAL but nonetheless scary. Like all neurotic fear, it has to be dealt with even though your rational mind may deny its force.

The fire-breathing dragon in fairy tales that attempts to burn up everything in her way is a metaphor for fear. To fight the dragon, you have to be a hero or heroine, in other words you have to live through pain, the pain of confronting and feeling fear and then acting over it.

Rilke writes: "We have no reason to mistrust our world for it is not against us. Has it terrors? They are our terrors. Has it abysses? Those abysses belong to us. Are dangers at hand? We must try to love them. And if only we arrange our life according to that principle which counsels us, that we must hold to the difficult (that is the heroism), then that which now seems to us the most alien will become what we most trust and find most faithful. How should we be able to forget those ancient myths—the myths about dragons that at the last moment turn into princesses? Perhaps all the dragons of our lives are princesses only waiting to see us once beautiful and brave. Perhaps everything terrible is in its deepest being something helpless that wants help from us." Everything that looked like such a dragon has within it this powerless-powerful princess who wants to be liberated.

Aikido works with the energy of the aggressor and turns that angry energy back onto an aggressor rather than coming at him with more violence. The Japanese word "irimi," used in Aikido training, means "entering." You enter the attack and you move toward it. You enter it in a non-invasive way. You blend with its energy with no attempt to oppose it, stop it, or strike back at it. That is exactly the way to work with fear. You feel the fear inside, enter into the feeling, and blend with it the way the tigers blended into butter in the story about Little Sambo. With no attempt to oppose, stop, or strike back, you meet the oncoming energy, and you experience it in its most intimate place, which is within your own soul. The energy of the attack gets folded back to resolution. This is the true meaning of integration, a combination of opposites: action that leads to repose.

You experience it rather than fight it. In other words, the it becomes I. There is no dualism. As long as we are trying to get rid of fear, we are not giving hospitality to something that is a deep part of our identity. Our ego identity includes a continual shuffling of fears and desires. When you face it and move into it instead of moving away from it, the moving becomes lively energy. Lively energy gives us the power to move through things, and we move through fear by entering its own energy. This is why our program in this book recommends not the rooting out of fear but the admitting and feeling of it in a self-compassionate way.

In keeping with our suggestion of handling fear gently: an authentic smile touches off synapses in the brain that make it impossible to feel fear. A smile cannot coexist with fear. If only you could smile at yourself for your neurotic fears, you would cancel out the fear for that moment. Letting go of the fear is not fighting it, but marrying it to something much more joyous and courageous.

TO DO: SIMPLE STEPS

There are three simple steps toward the handling of neurotic fear. Each of these steps should be preceded by a deep breath and calm abiding within an image that appeals to you and can relax you.

First, *admit* you feel fear. This breaks through all the rationalizations by which you talk yourself out of the fear or make it into something else. Instead of saying, "I am kind of uncomfortable around her," say, "I am afraid of her." Since our automatic reflex is to deny, a good rule of thumb might be to admit the fear even more fully than you feel it.

Second, *feel* the fear fully, i.e., defenselessly, with no escape, with no attempts to get rid of it. Shake, shudder, do whatever it takes for you to experience the emotion. Let this emotion stay in motion through you. *I let the fear go through me and I trust that the earth will receive and disperse it.* (Below you will find "The Allowing Technique" for a more detailed explanation of this step.)

Third, and most difficult, *act as if* fear could not stop you. I act as if I were fearless. This is the truth because I actually contain all opposites so I do have fearlessness inside me. It is only that I have not accessed it. I do not act from fear, I act with fear. (A courageous person is one who feels just as scared as you but *acts* bravely.) This plan adds resource-fullness to your defense-lessness.

When you follow these three steps, a shift occurs and you begin to trust that you really can live through fear. The reality is I am afraid. I honor that reality and admit it. That gesture is as real as the fear. Secondly, I feel it. That is real too. And thirdly, I act as if the fear did not hold me back. I do it anyway. That makes courage real. I have counterpoised reality to unreality, true evidence to false. The result is I become more heroic in my behavior and I notice that a shift occurs: I feel less and less fearful.

This shift makes me trust myself and enriches my self-respect. The energy that went into the elaborate fiction of rationalization and denial is reinvested in a new authenticity. What are the fictions? Every excuse you make to yourself, every because, every why, ever word in the dictionary except yes.

Admit, feel, and act is paradoxical because I am doing the very thing that I feared! I am fooling myself into health. "I am afraid of this, so I will do it." "I am afraid of this roller coaster, so let's buy the tickets." You trick yourself into getting over the fear. Jung says, "Only a paradox comes close to comprehending the fullness of life. Nonambiguity and noncontradictoriness, which the mind and logic love, are one-sided and could never express the miraculous."

Steps you employ lead to shifts that happen. The story of the Wizard of Oz does not begin with the confrontation with the witch in the castle of the flying monkeys. That most terrifying part comes at the end, after Dorothy has taken the steps to face the minor dragons. With each scary encounter, she becomes a little stronger and shifts into more power and more self-trust.

We began by saying that fear is refusal to integrate something. Now we are ready to understand the full meaning of this earlier statement. You fear the water and integrate it by learning to swim. How might you integrate fear? The way to integrate fear is to admit it, feel it, and act over it. Override it with your action. Do the very thing that you are afraid of. (In fact, Nietzsche says, "What does not kill you makes you stronger.")

EXAMPLE: FEAR OF SPEAKING UP FOR YOURSELF

First, admit: "I am afraid of speaking up." Your rationalizing mind may step in: "Wait a minute. It isn't that you can't speak up. It's that you do not want to hurt other people's feelings." Or, "If you speak up you might be rejected, so you'd better not." When you hear these inner inhibiting voices, you say, "Thank you for the information, and I admit I am afraid to speak up. Yes, I might hurt someone's feelings if I speak up. Yes, I might be rejected if I speak up. I *am* afraid of speaking up. And, since I am committed to a program of change, I will speak up, *while afraid*." Through these admissions, you are no longer a victim of your thoughts. You are not letting your mind get away with its intimidations or its rationalizations. You are answering fear with alternatives.

It helps to say these things aloud to someone. You may be wondering: why admit out loud that you feel afraid? Each admission whittles away at the ego and deflates its pretense of being in control. Since the neurotic ego is based on fear, the fear itself can then make room in your psyche that love will fill.

Secondly, you allow yourself to have the feeling itself. To the "act as if," the trickster mind may say, "You have admitted it and felt it—that is all you have to do. Give yourself the reward of dropping it." But instead you say, "I am going to risk speaking up anyway." At the decision to do this, at this moment between feeling and acting as if, you will feel the shift, a surge of power to take that final step. There is something about every step that empowers you to take one more. This is where the mind finally gives up because it sees you *doing it* and cannot stop you anymore. Now you are no longer the victim because you have combined vulnerability: "I might fail," with power: "I am doing it."

Thirdly, I act as if I were not fearful. I make the choices I would make if I did not feel the fear. A good question to ask yourself is: "What would I do if I were not afraid?" "Acting as if," throughout the day, throughout the week, throughout the year, builds a bridge to fearlessness. It is a neuronal highway. This is how you can change the messages in your brain, creating a highway to freedom from the cellular fear. Since fear is encoded in us physiologically, freedom from it requires a bodily change. Every time you act as if you were not afraid, you instruct your cells to let go of fear. Every time you rationalize

it away and do not act, the fear is instructed to leave everything as it is. We are never free from fear entirely, but we are
free from being gripped by the neurotic story lines that surround the fear and make us so ashamed and powerless that
we cannot handle it. That is true freedom from fear.

*I began with the fear of speaking up. I said no to all the ration-
alizations and I moved into something that empowered me. Now I
can see that the integration of fear is actually a hero's journey from
living in fear, being stuck in fear, to moving through fear.*

THE ALLOWING TECHNIQUE: PAUSING FOR
FEELING OUR FEAR

Give fear room, a hearing, and a cradle:

Before you try to fix it, you have to let it happen fully.

Make room and time, tune in to what you are feeling,
    and hold/cradle it, i.e., grant it legitimacy.

Then something opens and you are empowered.

Picture the father who stops what he is doing to listen to
the whimpering child and squats down to his level and tunes
in and hugs the child in his pain. Then the child feels better
and runs off with an enlarged sense of his own power.

To have to become different only destroys self-esteem.
Real courage is not in rooting out but in delving into, a stark
encounter with our fear. Then feelings are neither positive nor
negative but all neutral, like waves at high or low tide yet
always moving. Feelings are always flowing in us though we
do not see them—as waves are flowing now but we are not
watching them. When something happens, we are dragged to
the beach and notice the waves! The hero is not one who elim-

inates fear but one who finds a way through it, by feeling it, facing it, and over-riding its tendency to stop him.

When I feel afraid or bereft or lonely, I admit it and let myself feel it, capturing the unique felt sense of it, connecting it to childhood pain that resembles it. I brood on my own chaos as the Holy Spirit brooded over the dark waters of creation.

I sit in my fear and forlornness, without running to my usual hide-outs: call someone, turn on the TV, look for sex, eat, drink alcohol, take a tranquilizer, etc. When I grant hospitality to myself, I need no other guest.

The more I let myself feel my feelings, the more do I expand my capacity to feel. This is how I nurture myself effectively so I am less likely to look for anybody to fulfill me or fill me. As I service myself this way, I need him/her to service my neediness less and less. Now I can love needlessly.

Love will no longer mean: you are the right size doll for my cut-out collection, but: you are who you are and I correctly assess and respect your dimensions. I no longer adorn or embellish them for my own needy purpose of denying or fleeing my ultimate loneliness. Objects of addiction and clinging (people or things) become less appealing as I take care of myself. Self-parenting is thus self-liberation.

We will never get over our fear until we love ourselves. When we open to our feelings, our hearts are soft and accessible to ourselves and to others. That self-accepted heart is the sanctuary of fearlessness. Fearlessness is not less fear or no fear but so much more love that we go beyond fear at last. Fear is the porcupine you see on the trail as you hike: interesting to you but not stopping you and not to be eliminated since it belongs to the ecology of the psychic path.

What we are holding may be inconsolable based on authentic inconsolable experiences of childhood. Self-parenting does not fix or reverse that given of our life. It remains like an old scar: irreversible and yet not damaging.

New losses that in any way resemble it may trigger a

panic to fix it. In a relationship in which you are projecting a father imago onto a partner, an abandonment by that partner will carry the original pain of the loss of father. We desperately want that person not to leave us because of the great emotional torment at stake: "Console me by staying! Do not let me feel the full brunt of the original inconsolability!"

No amount of self-parenting or therapy can reverse or eliminate the inconsolable part of us. True health is in accepting the irreversibility of the inconsolability. This, too, is gentle work, not eliminating but allowing. Paradoxically, freedom happens to us when we no longer look for consolation of the inconsolable in anybody or anything. Just as the Sahara does not hurt this planet by its unrelieved barrenness, so our deserted places do not disturb the ecology of our psyche. It would be wrong to bring visitors there in order to make it into a theme park!

A ruthless acknowledgment of what life did to me and an acceptance of the part of it that does not change leads to healing, paradoxically. Remember how Demeter grieves the loss of Persephone and thereby brings to mankind the gift of grain.

Am I in a relationship safe enough to hold myself this way? Can my partner hold me?

Compare these two images to see the integration of this work:

Moses floats down the unwelcoming waters of the Nile: above him the void of the sky, below him the void of the deep river. He does not do anything. He simply lies in his basket; he simply stays there experiencing the orphan's poignant pain, expecting nothing, despairing nothing. Among the bulrushes, he is lifted by a princess to a nurtured life.

Now see the disciples in the storm on the sea of Galilee, threatened with drowning in the tempestuous waves, fruitlessly using every sailor's trick and skill to save themselves (how the ego tries to become whole by will power and not by grace!). Jesus is walking toward them on the waters, calming the storm as he says: "Be not afraid: it is I."

The two positions comprise the work: we lie down and let the fear carry us where it wants to go and later we walk on the very waves that scared us before. We let fear happen and then we are carried by it to serenity.

The fear that seems like an IT: separate from us, against us, split off from us and opposing us is really part of us: "IT is I!" This is why Freud said that healing meant: "Where it was, there I shall be." When it is I, there opens a moment of freedom from it. This is fearlessness. Fear is a given of the human psyche and therefore somehow useful and transformative, if we ride it rather than let it trample us.

> *The mind of fearfulness*
> *Should be put into the cradle of loving-kindness*
> *And suckled with the milk of freedom from self-doubt...*
> *Then the fearful mind*
> *Can change into the warrior's mind,*
> *And that eternally youthful confidence*
> *Can expand into the space without beginning or end.*
> *At that point, it sees the Great Rising Eastern Sun of*
> *   human goodness.*
> —Tibetan Shambhala Poem

When Carrie Left Patrick

Carrie and Patrick were married for ten years when Carrie suddenly announced that she had been involved with another man for the past six months and now would be leaving Patrick for him. Patrick was devastated and broken-hearted. He had trusted Carrie so implicitly! This infidelity was a great shock and he wanted more than anything to get Carrie back. He begged her to return to him, but she was adamant and even arrogant in her manner to him. Nothing could change her mind, certainly not Patrick's pain. Meanwhile, Patrick lost his appetite, could not sleep, became obsessed with Carrie, and deeply mourned her loss. All he could believe was that, if Carrie would return, all would be fine again.

Patrick consulted a therapist who helped him see that he was taking the loss too literally and narrowly: it was not just abut Carrie, it was about all the women who had left or betrayed him in the course of his life. "In fact," said the therapist, "obsession is a signal that the object of our obsession is actually a metaphor for something that is unresolved within us, usually from our childhood! We take our partners in adult life literally when they are more often figurative."

Patrick became aware of the many ways his own mother had abandoned him from early life: by her emotional distance from him and her lack of real interest in his emotional experience. He saw that his loss was bigger than Carrie. In fact, the enormity of his reaction could not be accounted for by the loss of Carrie!

Patrick became more honest with himself. At first, he had embellished and inflated the value of his relationship with Carrie. He realized now that the relationship had really been a source of unhappiness for him in many ways. He began to see that the part of him that wanted her back was the needy, bereft, abandoned child. The part of him that was ready to let her go was the adult who recognized the wisdom in the ending, though also the unkindness in it. Patrick saw that he was grieving the loss of something that was not there: a warmth and safety that he had never actually found in Carrie. His pain was not about how valuable a relationship was disappearing but about how hard it was to let go of something that had become a comfortable habit! Carrie was actually helping Patrick as he thought more about it. After all, he could not let go of what did not work, he could not let go of what he did not want! "Carrie won't give me what I don't want. She is setting limits on me that I cannot set on myself!" He found himself feeling lucky and even thankful to both Carrie and her new partner! But the grief and pain remained, insisting on its time.

Gradually, Patrick began simply to sit with the feelings of despondency, sadness, and loneliness without doing anything at all about them. He simply experienced his feelings; he paid attention to them as neither his mother nor Carrie had ever done. He mirrored himself. He held his feelings and changed the face in his mind from that of Carrie to that of his mother and to the faces of all the women who had left him. In this way, he grieved all his female losses, piggy-backing onto one another. Finally, he saw his own face and realized that he had abandoned himself by fleeing his feelings and staying in relationships of unhappiness and inadequacy.

At the same time, he finally was allowing himself to feel starkly and fully, with the depth he was always capable of but had long suppressed. This expanded his capacity to feel more richly. Patrick now knew himself better and liked himself more! He was nurturing himself more generously and giving to himself the love and holding that he had missed from his mother and from Carrie and from himself. He continued to follow this simple path of staying with his feelings and no longer applying them as literally as about Carrie. His new-found strength and deeper contact with his feelings had the effect of making her less appealing! Why would he want someone who could not provide what he needed and now could provide for himself?

Patrick did not run to a new relationship. He enjoyed his own company for a long time. Someday he will relate in a healthier way than was ever possible for him before. Carrie had helped him find himself and love's meaning. Their marriage had worked.

TO DO: TAKING AN INVENTORY

> *Fear no more the frown of the great,*
> *Thou art past the tyrant's stroke.*
> —Cymbeline

It is now clear that each of us feels afraid often. It is understandable that fear is so pervasive in our lives. For one thing, we live in a world that is so often scary! And secondly, most of us were raised in atmospheres of fear. We absorbed fear before we had the chance to say No to it. We are now facing our program of recovery from fear.

Fear may convince us that the worst will happen and that we will be unable to handle it. This is the powerlessness that makes fear so sinister. We rally our power with the conviction that there is an alternative to what the frightened mind has construed and that we do have it within us to handle whatever comes our way.

You may find this worksheet helpful in taking a personal inventory of your fears and in designing affirmations to clear fears. It also serves as a mini-course on fear! It combines the three elements of fearwork: admitting fear, feeling it fully, and acting as it we were fearless.

Read it onto a tape and listen to it daily in your own voice or recite or read it regularly. Form an image of yourself acting out each affirmation you recite. This list (like all the lists in this book) is meant for a wide audience, so add or delete entries to fit your unique situation:

I trust my true fears to give me signals of danger.

I admit that I also have false fears and worries.

I feel compassion toward myself for all the years I have been afraid.

I forgive those who hypnotized me into unreal fears.

I suggest now to myself, over and over, that I am freeing myself from fear.

I have fearlessness to match my fear.

I trust my powers and resourcefulness as a man (woman).

I trust my abundant creativity.

I trust the strength that opens and blooms in me when I have to face something.

I believe in myself as a man/woman who handles what comes his/her way today.

I know how to rise to a challenge.

I am more and more aware of how I hold fear in my body.

I stop storing fear in my body.

Now I relax those holding places.

I open my body to joy and serenity.

I release my body from the clench of fear.

I relax the part of me that holds fear the most (jaw, shoulders, neck, etc.).

I let go of the stress and tension that come from fear.

I let go of fear-based thoughts.

I let go of basing my decisions on fear.

I stop listening to those who want to import their fears into me.

I let go of finding something to fear in everything.

I let go of fear and fearing and of believing that everything is fearsome.

I let go of my primitive ways of catastrophizing (e.g., a fear belief: it is going to stay this way!).

I am more and more aware of my instant reflex fear reactions.

I am aware that I have habituated myself to a certain level of adrenaline.

I admit that I (sometimes) (often) (always) choose the adrenaline rush that comes with the dramas of fear and desire.

I forego this stressful excitement and choose sane and serene liveliness.

I let go of my obsessive thoughts about how the worst may happen.

I trust myself always to find an alternative.

I see the humor in my fears.

I see the humor in my exaggerated reactions to unreal dangers.

I find a humorous dimension in every fear.

I find a humorous response for every fear.

I play with the pain of fear.

I smile at my scared ego with tough love.

I am confident in my ability to deal with situations or people that scare me.

I am more and more aware of how everything that happens or has happened is being faced, integrated, and let go of.

I have self-healing powers—and—I seek and find support outside myself.

I have an enormous capacity for re-building, restoring, transcending.

I am more and more sure of my abilities.

I am less and less scared by what happens, by what has happened, by what will happen.

I trust myself.

I trust an uncanny timing that I keep noticing within myself:

I love how I awake or change or resolve or complete at just the right moment.

Nothing forces me; nothing stops me.

I let go of any fear I have of nature.

I let go of my fears of natural disasters.

I let go of my fears of sickness, accident, old age, and death.

I cease being afraid of knowing, having or showing my feelings.

I let go of my fear of failure or of success.

I let go of the fear behind my guilt and shame.

I let go of my fear of aloneness or of time on my hands.

I let go of my fear of abandonment.

I let go of my fear of engulfment.

I let go of my fear of closeness.

I let go of my fear of commitment.

I let go of my fear of being betrayed.

I let go of my fear of being cheated or robbed.

I let go of my fears of giving/receiving, beginnings/endings, comings/goings, scarcity/abundance, saying No/saying Yes.

I let go of my fear of any person.

I let go of my fear of loving.

I let go of my fear of being loved.

I let go of the fear that I will lose, lose money, lose face, lose freedom, lose friends, lose family members, lose respect, lose status, lose my job, lose out.

I let go of my fear of having to grieve.

I keep letting go and I keep going on.

I let go of my paranoia.

I give up my phobic rituals.

I let go of my performance fears.

I let go of my sexual fears.

I let go of fears about my adequacy as a parent or child, as a worker or manager, as a partner or friend.

I let go of the need to be in control.

I acknowledge control as a mask for my fear.

I let go of my need to be right, to be first, to be perfect.

I let go of my belief that I am entitled to be taken care of.

I let go of my fear of the conditions of existence:

>   I accept that I may sometimes lose;
>
>   I accept that things change and end;
>
>   I accept that pain is part of human growth;
>
>   I accept that things are not always fair;
>
>   I accept that people may lie to me, betray me, or not be loyal to me.

I am flexible enough to accept life as it is, forgiving enough to accept it as it has been.

I drop the need for or belief in a personal exemption from the conditions of my existence.

I acknowledge my present predicament as a path.

I trust a design in spite of the display.

I let go of more than any fate can take.

I appreciate all the ways that things work out for me.

I appreciate the graces that everywhere surround and enrich my life.

I find the alternatives that always exist behind the apparent dead-end of fear.

I open myself to the flow of life and people and events.

I am grateful for the love that awaits me everywhere.

I feel deeply loved by many people near and far, living and dead.

I feel loved and watched over by a higher power (God, Universe, etc.).

I believe that I have an important destiny, that I am living in accord with it, and that I will survive to fulfill it.

I let myself have the full measure of:

> the joy I was meant to feel,

> the joy of living without fear.

I let fear go and let joy in.

I let fear go and let love in.

I let go of fears and enlarge my sympathies.

I am more and more aware of others' fears, more and more sensitive to them, more and more compassionate toward them.

I am more and more acceptant of all kinds of people.

I enlarge my circle of love to include every living being: I show my love.

I am more and more courageous as I live my program for dealing with fear:

> I let go of control;
>
> I let the chips fall where they may;
>
> I admit my fear;
>
> I feel my fear by letting it pass through me;
>
> I act as if I were free of fear;
>
> I enjoy the humor in my fears;
>
> I expand my compassion toward myself and everyone.

I have pluck and wit.

I let go of being on the defensive.

I protect myself.

I am nonviolent.

I am intrepid under fire.

I am a hero: I live through pain and am transformed by it.

I am undaunted by people or circumstances that may threaten me.

I let people's attempts to menace me fall flat.

I give up running from threats.

I give up shrinking from a fight.

I show grace under pressure.

I stop running; I stop hiding.

More and more of my fear is becoming healthy excitement.

I meet danger face to face.

I stand up to a fight.

I take the bull by the horns.

I run the gauntlet.

I put my head in the lion's mouth.

I stick to my guns and hold my fire.

An automatic courage arises in me when I *face* a threat.

I dare to show myself as I am: afraid *and* courageous.

I hereby release the courage that has lain hidden within me.

I am thankful for the gift of fortitude.

I let go of hesitation and self-doubt.

I am hardy in the face of fear.

I have grit, stamina, and toughness.

I take risks and always act with responsibility and grace.

I let go of the fear of being different.

I let go of the need to meet others' expectations.

I cease being intimidated by others' anger.

I let go of my fear of what may happen if people do not like me.

I let go of my fear of false accusations.

I let go of having to do it his/her/their way.

I acknowledge that behind my exaggerated sense of obligation is a fear of my own freedom.

I let go of my terror about disapproval, ridicule, or rejection.

I dare to stop auditioning for people's approval.

I dare to give up my act.

I give up all my poses, pretenses, and posturings.

I dare to be myself.

I acknowledge that behind my fear of self-disclosure is a fear of freedom.

I dare to show my hand, to show my inclinations, to show my enthusiasms.

I let my every word, feeling, and deed reveal me as I truly am.

I love being found out, i.e., caught in the act of being my authentic self.

I explore the farthest reaches of my identity.

I dare to live the life that truly reflects my deepest needs and wishes.

I give up the need to correct people's impressions of me.

I give up being afraid of my own power.

I am irrepressible.

I draw upon ever-renewing sources of lively energy within me.

I am great-hearted and bold-spirited.

I dare to give of myself unconditionally—and—

I dare to be unconditionally committed to maintaining my own boundaries.

I am open to the grace that shows me the difference.

I fling open the gates of my soul.

I set free my love, till now imprisoned by fear.

I set free my joy, till now imprisoned by fear.

I honor and evoke my animal powers, my human powers, my divine powers.

I let true love cast out my fear.

I face fear as Buddha did; I am Buddha in the face of fear.

> *For all that has been: Thanks!*
> *For all that will be: Yes!*
> —Dag Hammarskjöld

Once while Buddha was sitting under the Bodhi tree, his enemies set a wild white elephant charging at him. He raised his right hand, palm outward to heart-level and cupped his left hand, palm upward, at waist-level. He thereby silently stated "No to fear!" with his right hand and "Yes to love!" with his left hand. Both messages were directed to the elephant, who became serene and tame and bowed to the Buddha. This was the first Mudra: a hand positioning that is a form of meditation leading to a calm abiding in fearlessness. (Mudra means seal, i.e., make deep impression.)

> *The only way to say no to fear is to say yes to love.*
> *The only way to say yes to love is to say no to fear.*

6.

Becoming More Courageous

_____

There came a time when staying tight with the bud
became more painful than the risk it took to bloom.
                                        —Anaïs Nin

This bud of love, by summer's ripening breath
Shall become a beauteous flower when next we meet.
                                        —Romeo and Juliet

It is now clear that any power fear can have over us comes from the belief that we have no alternative. What we truly fear is finding ourselves without recourse: trapped and defeated. The instant we see a new path, we feel powerful and joyous. This is the single-most significant way to liberate ourselves from the grip of fear. Where are the alternatives we can choose? Assertiveness shows us a way to become powerful in facing the situation or person that is scaring us. To find a powerful place to stand is to let go of fear.

Acting assertively, i.e., courageously, displaces our fear. Passive, non-assertive behavior keeps us fear-based. Aggressive behavior originates in our own fear and instills fear in others. Assertive behavior is exactly how we "act as if." In this chapter, we use exercises and practical step by step examples that show how to handle fear and raise self-esteem at the same time.

Assertiveness—is another word for power, and it is defined the same way:

167

- Being clear about who you are and what you are up to,

- Asking for what you want,

- Taking responsibility for your feelings and behavior.

Notice the achievability, the accessibility of these components.

This contrasts with the scared ego's way of looking at power:

- Being sure of everything,

- Getting what you want,

- Having others take care of you and cover your errors.

Not all of us can achieve the latter; in fact, few of us can. Defining power as having, rather than being, makes it an elitist experience. In handling fear by assertiveness, we are learning to recognize personal power as truly available to us. This is how it provides an immediate boost to our self-esteem.

There is an empowering, invigorating feeling associated with *clarity*. This differs from the insecurity and alienation associated with being right all the time. Clarity about who you are is a declaration to others of your identity as you know it. It includes fearless proclamation that you are discernible and candid, not in hiding! This chosen visibility paradoxically supplants your fear of disclosure!

Asking for what you want means: showing others who you are and what you need, as well as taking care of yourself by asking. This breaks through so much early training in passivity!

Taking responsibility for the shape your life has taken and for the consequences of every choice you have made resonates as a sense of personal power in that you are the active maker of your own life. When others take care of you, when they pay your fines, you are letting yourself be defined as a victim, helpless to negotiate the turns on your own path.

There are four presuppositions to assertiveness:

The first is that you do have power over your responses. You do not have to walk away from situations, saying to yourself, "If only I had said...." You can practice and learn how to be in touch with your feelings so that when a situation arises, you will be able to respond to it in ways that you find satisfactory.

The second presupposition is that you do not have to wait until your attitude changes in order to start changing your behavior. Behavior can change before attitudes. Attitudes will follow suit. You can *act as if* you were assertive without having to wait until you build up enough self-confidence for it.

The third presupposition is that assertiveness can be achieved gradually. We build from the easy experiences to the more difficult. We do not begin by saying, "I want a separation." We begin by saying, "Let's talk about what this relationship feels like."

The final presupposition is that expressing one's feelings is a safe, non-violent method of interacting with others. Aggressive behavior occurs because we hold in anger and fear, not because we let it out. Aggression is an explosion; assertiveness is an even, smooth release.

To Do: Asserting Our Fearlessness by Acting As If

I. CLARITY

• Showing Your Hand

Having clarity involves being open about who you are, what you are feeling, and what your intentions are. To be clear is to show what you are up to, what you mean by what you are saying. It is the opposite of "playing it close to the vest," being guarded or defensive: "No matter how well you bluff, eventually you will have to lay your cards on the table."

- BEING ABLE TO SAY YES, NO, OR MAYBE
When you want to say yes, say yes; when you want to say no, say no; and when you want to say maybe, say maybe. Being assertive does not mean being sure; it means having clarity.

- HAVING AN INTEGRAL SENSE OF SELF
Use your body as an echo chamber, taking cues from it. The body never lies. If every time you perform a certain behavior, you get a headache, that behavior is not good for you. An assertive person does what feels good all over. He never responds to some driving message in his mind when his body is telling him that is not the thing to do.

- BEING SPECIFIC
"Do not tell me you will love me forever; tell me you will love me on Thursday afternoon at 4 o'clock," said W.H. Auden. Be specific about what you need. For instance, "I do not trust you" is an assertive statement, but it is too general. If you say instead, "I do not trust you; here is what I need to trust you," you are getting more specific. When you present specific ingredients that would make things better for you, you are saying, "I do not want things to stay this way. I want to change them for the better."

- GIVING CLEAR MESSAGES
An example: somebody wants to borrow your car, and you do not want to loan it. Give a clear message by saying assertively, "I make it a policy not to loan my car." A non-assertive response would be: "I can't lend you my car today because I have to go to the bank." In this latter example, the other person might ask you again because he did not under-

stand the true message: you did not want to lend it. You then resent him for asking. The result is not clear and powerful communication, but a cramped, uneasy struggle.

- BEING AWARE OF YOUR NEEDS

This presumes first accepting that you have needs at all. For instance, isolated people sometimes refuse to let themselves look at their loneliness. They do not reach out to others but remain isolated. Awareness and clarity, in this instance, would require breaking through the inertia and admitting, "I am lonely." Then the way would be opened for the next awareness: "What do I need to feel better?" Awareness is a process with steps. We move from awareness, to mobilization, to taking the action that makes for change. But we only do the second step when we have let ourselves do the first.

II. ASKING FOR WHAT YOU WANT

- ASKING FOR CLEAR MESSAGES

"Tell me what you really mean" is preferable to being left with doubts or guessing someone's meaning. Asking for what you want includes inquiring into another's agenda: "You've asked me to a candlelight dinner; are you perhaps looking for romance?"

Asking for clear messages may also involve asking for ground rules in relationships. For instance, you might say, "I would like to have a ground rule in this relationship that if either of us becomes involved with anybody else sexually, he or she will tell the other about it." These statements seem embarrassing to make. Embarrassment is another word for fear. A willingness to be embarrassed and awkward is a prerequisite for change.

- CHECKING THINGS OUT

Assertiveness involves checking out one's personal fantasies, doubts, and intuitions. For example, if you were wondering what was going on between your partner and a co-worker of his, rather than hiring an investigator, you would ask for yourself. If his answer seems like a cover-up, you may say, "I do not believe that," or "That's hard to grasp. Can you help me understand why I feel this way? My intuition says that you are getting involved, yet you say no. Let's keep talking."

Sometimes a person will not validate your intuition and you say to yourself, "What's wrong with me? Why am I not seeing this as it is?" For instance, "You used to call me every week; now you do not call me at all. Has something happened that changed our friendship?" "No, everything's fine," the other person says. This is an example of not having your intuition validated. It is crazy-making because you are thinking to yourself, "Why did I come up with my interpretation? What's wrong with me?" Actually you were probably correct. "I still trust my intuition," you may say, "and I would like to talk more about it." You are thereby trusting what you are feeling and making a move toward the truth.

- VALIDATING

Anytime you express a feeling to someone, you may ask if it has been comprehended. Has what you have said been heard? Being validated differs from being justified. It refers to being appreciated, endorsed, or at least understood. For instance, someone may say, "I resent that you do not do as much of the work around here as we originally agreed you would do." The validation for that is not, "What do you mean? I do just as much as you." Rather it might be something like this: "I understand how you feel and I will get on the ball." That is validation. When there is no validation, try the broken-record technique: repeating what you say until you are understood and heard.

- ASKING FOR APPRECIATION OR COMPLIMENTS

Appreciation and compliments are personal recognitions expressed verbally or physically. The assertive person asks for positive feedback and appreciation. He knows he needs it and seeks it directly. This involves asking for recognition or credit for what he has accomplished or tenderness and physical intimacy when he feels the need for it.

III. TAKING RESPONSIBILITY

• ACCEPTING THE ASSERTIONS OF OTHERS

Assertiveness is a two-way street. It is an interactional experience that makes you intent on the messages others are conveying to you about themselves. This involves not only a willingness to hear others, but a genuine respect for who they are and what they want. It involves sensitivity to the needs and feelings of others. True intimacy attends to the being of another person and the existential demands of the moment you are sharing. It is knowing that this is the moment to be kind, that other obligations can wait. By being awake to the smothered sobs, frightened silences, or silent screams you become attuned to the other. This is what it means to care.

• RESPONDING TO IMPACT

Assertiveness involves responding to the impact of one's experiences, not just to another's intention. For example, someone snubs you at work, and you say to yourself, "Oh well, he must be in a bad mood." You excuse it and do not mention it. You have responded to an intention in someone's head which you have opined. A more appropriate way to respond might be, "I realize you're in a bad mood, but you hurt my feelings when you snubbed me." If you were to say this, you would be *responding to the impact while acknowledging the intention.* In this instance, you would be taking responsibility for your feelings and still kindly staying aware of someone else's hard place. Of course, when the distress is extreme, you may choose to forego mentioning your feelings. For example, if you heard harsh words expressed by someone just stricken with grief, the better part of love would call for

silence. Love and caring often demand our not acting assertively, in fact.

Generally, you are not hurting someone's feelings when
you are declaring your own feelings. You hurt others' feelings
when the "I" statements of personal feeling become the "you"
statements of reproach or judgment. When you state your
feelings and hear: "You hurt my feelings," you can validate
the other's feelings by saying, "I believe you feel hurt. I'm
sharing my feelings with you and would like to have them
heard, just the same." Acknowledge the reality of the hurt,
while still asking for a hearing.

- EXPRESSING FEELINGS

In assertiveness we are taking responsibility for feelings
whether easy (e.g., joy) or painful (e.g., fear) by owning them.
We are letting ourselves experience all our feelings rather
than covering them up. There are no negative feelings, only
hard ones to experience. Assertiveness means accepting the
tender and the hard parts of yourself. Accept the fact that you
are vulnerable, caring, concerned, giving. Accept the fact that
at some levels you are greedy or selfish or vindictive, etc. Part
of this is accepting our negative shadow, the features of ourselves that we disown and try not to be aware of. A way to
find our own negative shadow is to examine what we cannot
abide in others!

It is difficult to express our feelings and sometimes they
are so blocked in us (or stored in our muscles as tensions) that
we need therapy to free them up. Our bodies are the visual
image of our feelings. The assertive person lets go of these
hold-outs and shows others what he is feeling.

Intimacy is sharing feelings, not just data or even secrets.
We may find it easier to tell someone something about ourselves that we are ashamed of than to show our feelings of
shame. Freeing up these inhibited styles of communication is
equivalent to taking responsibility for what we are feeling
and is perhaps the most threatening feature of assertiveness.

Beauty could not accept the Beast because of his ugliness and finally, at the moment of his death, she shed a tear for him; she showed feeling for him, and he turned into a prince. Every negative feeling that is in us will turn into something beautiful once we acknowledge it and accept it. Frowning faces may even smile at us.

• Finishing Unfinished Emotional Business
"Two years ago we had a fight, and we haven't spoken since. I would like to be friends again. I would like to go over what happened, hear your resentment, express mine and be done with this so that we can go on to a new level in our friendship."

The end of a relationship or friendship is a loss that needs to be mourned. Even a relationship that was brief or that you chose to leave will have residual feelings of loss and grief that require attention. The assertive person will not run from this work into another relationship immediately or into oblivion through dependency on chemicals. Instead of distraction and consolation, he will mourn the loss on his own or in therapy or even directly with the person involved. When the timing is right (feels good all over!) he will recontact the other and work things out. Nothing can force an assertive person to act prematurely; nothing can stop him once the time has come.

• Being Socially Aware
We looked at the issue of self-awareness in the section on being clear. The other aspect of this experience is social awareness, a sense of the interface of my needs and those of the greater society. The assertive person will take responsibility for the consequences of his acts. He realizes that his needs and choices do not exist in a vacuum, but exist in concert with the needs and rights of others. The assertive person works out a way of need-fulfillment that respects these rights and, when he trespasses on them, makes amends. This is psychological ecology!

PASSIVITY: GIVING POWER AWAY
BECAUSE OF FEAR:
WHAT NOT TO DO

Power is either owned (assertiveness), given away (non-assertiveness, passivity), or used to discount or control (aggressiveness). Nobody takes power away from us; we hand it over. Here are the characteristic styles of passive, fear-based, nonassertive behavior:

- APOLOGIES AND EXCUSES

As stated above, an excuse for other people is often the pay-off for not having to confront the behavior that is disturbing us. We may perform mental surgery on experiences so that we can gain closure on them without having to feel the inner trepidation that may be associated with an assertion on our part.

If someone hurts my feelings, I can close the issue for myself by saying (inwardly), "He doesn't know any better," or "He's that way with everyone," or "Why make things uneasy between us? Let it slide by for now." Instead of making excuses or accepting excuses, we act assertively when we use an "I" statement that declares the impact of the feeling on us: "I feel hurt by what you said."

- COPING

A nonassertive life-style is one in which more than half the time is spent coping. "Patience" is the Latin word for suffering; "endurance" is the word for hardening. We are choosing to suffer and to hold on to the status quo when we invest our energy in coping. The opposite of coping is changing. *Whatever is not changed is chosen.* Complaining and whining are usually characteristic of people who do not want to change things. The wife of the alcoholic who complains about her husband's repeated drunkenness and yet makes excuses to his boss when he is not at work is being nonassertive. The assertive response is to stop complaining about him and stop covering for him while finding ways to take care of herself.

- SMOOTHING OVER
The nonassertive person tends to smooth over situations so that anger does not erupt. "I have to treat this person with kid gloves because he easily flies off the handle." The nonassertive person will excuse this, preserving the "peace" by placating or disregarding. Actually this is acting against the truth. The other person is truly belligerent or angry or explosive. The nonassertive cloak over the behavior does not permit the truth to emerge. This is a very reasonable strategy with a violent or insane person but a losing proposition with a person you are relating to.

- INHIBITION
Inhibition is fear of doing what we really want to do. It is *not* acting because of what might or should not happen. "Happen" is the opposite of "do." The nonassertive person thinks of things happening to him rather than of having the power to do something about what may happen. "I do not want to go out and meet people because I'm afraid (so I'll stay here and be lonely)." The first clause of this sentence is quite assertive; it admits fear. The parenthetic phrase is non-assertive since it means remaining stuck in fear.

- LIVING REACTIVELY
Sometimes our behavior and/or feelings are based on what others may do. This is nonassertive because the power is in the hands of someone else. She makes the decisions. I then plan my strategy. Strategizing is nonassertive behavior since it is attempts to prevent or control a reality rather than letting it unfold: this is acting against the truth. The parents who are constantly bailing out their drug-dependent daughter are living reactively. They are giving up their own life in favor of rescuing her—and harming her in the process.

"We're letting you now take responsibility for what you do. Deal with the consequences of your acts as you choose. We offer you support in getting the therapy you need for change and no more than that." This would be a nonreactive (assertive) response to a delinquent son or daughter.

• OVER-COMMITMENT
This is the burn-out syndrome, well described as doing too much for too long for too little with no thanks. When more demands are put upon you, you meet them with even more effort! It applies to jobs and relationships.

• CONSTANT GIVING IN
Healthy adults seek negotiation followed by a mutually acceptable agreement. The accent is not on giving up what you want, but on making agreements wherein each person receives something that she wants. When you are giving in more than half the time, you are living a compromised life.

• ACTING AS GO-BETWEEN
"I'll speak to your father for you. I think I can convince him." This is living out someone else's responsibility. Whenever I act for you, I thereby give up my chance of acting for myself. There is a fine line between this and rescue, a form of aggression. What makes this nonassertive rather than aggressive is that the emphasis is on not taking care of yourself. It is caretaking at the expense of self-assertion.

• OVER-POLITENESS
Politeness is a gracious style of behavior. Over-politeness means letting others be first most of the time. I am waiting in line and someone gets ahead of me. I am embarrassed or too polite to speak up. Over-politeness—as we saw earlier —was invented to legitimize embarrassed nonassertiveness.

• PLAYING UNDERDOG
This refers to approaching people like a "little boy with hat in hand." You feel that just because they have something that you want, they are thereby above you and can intimidate you. You try to say only what will please them or what will show them your worthiness. Conversations with bosses, judges, police, etc., are often in this category. "Even though I've been speeding, I still want to be treated with the respect due a citizen." "Even though you are my supervisor, I still want to talk freely, person-to-person. My role as an employee does not cancel my right to respect and equality."

AGGRESSION: WHEN POWER BECOMES CONTROL: WHAT NOT TO DO

In assertiveness you own your power, in non-assertiveness you give it away, in aggressiveness you use it in a controlling way. "I do not like this professor; I do not want to go to his class. I'm going to tell him what an awful teacher he is." This is actively aggressive—telling him off and putting him down, rather than telling him how you feel about the class and about your distress. You could also approach this passively by simply not going to class, showing up late, or causing problems while in class, behaviors which are passive-aggressive. Usually a passive-aggressive style can be interpreted in more than one way. It can be interpreted as "I'm simply late," or "I do not like the class." Most of us use the passive-aggressive style because it involves fewer confrontations. An examination of eight types of aggressive behavior shows precisely the difference between assertiveness and aggressiveness:

• PUT-DOWNS
Instead of saying, "I am angry at you," you say, "I'm angry at you; you're such an idiot." The first sentence is assertive because you expressed a feeling; the second was aggressive because a judgment was added. (This is the drama

that is the opposite of assertiveness.) The second part of the statement might lead to an argument and animosity while the first part might have led to communication.

"You" statements, e.g., "You have no sense of fair play," are generally aggressive because they involve verdicts based on judgments. "I" statements, e.g., "I feel anger at this unfair treatment," are generally assertive since they are simply declarations of what you are feeling or how you are reacting to a person, word, or behavior. When Christ said, "Call no man a fool," he was not proposing politeness but truth. No one is a fool. No one is one-down. Only those who fear for their own inferiority need to put others down. This is operating from internal defensiveness and is usually expressed in external aggression.

• Manipulation

Manipulating is a strategy for getting something from someone that he does not want to give up or even notice he is giving it up. It is aggressive, as it seeks to control others and discount their rights. Manipulation might be evident in guilt-tripping or power plays: threats; storming out in the midst of an argument so that the other person is left high and hot; the silent treatment.

• Blaming

Blaming is based on the need to be right and to make the other person wrong. It usually masks a demand to do something "my way." It is aggressive because it is the opposite of clear communication and attempts to put the other person down.

• Projecting Responsibility

"You made me angry." "Look what you made me do." "If it hadn't been for you, I would have…" When responsibility is projected onto someone else, it is done in an accusatory, vindictive, petulant way. All this opposes the assertive style in which I say, "I'm angry; here's what it is about…" or, "I realize my anger is my responsibility and you haven't caused it. Part of my taking responsibility for it is telling you about it." A great percentage of what we are feeling may be touched off by the behavior of someone else but dealing with the feeling is not her responsibility. "I'm painfully aware of your part in what I feel, but my feelings are my own. I ask only that you help me work through them." Taking responsibility while pointing out others' contributions to what you feel is assertive.

• RESCUE

The victim has literally been put in the down position and will be angry about it, as all persecuted people are. His anger will be mobilized against his rescuer and he will become the persecutor. Rescuing, as seen above, is doing more than half the work, putting in more than half the effort, for somebody else. You are thus rendering the other helpless. Another word for rescuer is "victimizer." You are not giving help; you are fostering helplessness and resentment. Whenever I take care of someone else by doing for her what she can do for herself, I am keeping her one-down in the guise of "helping." The aggression here is twofold: from rescuer to victim and from persecutor back to rescuer again.

• COMPETITION

We saw the distinction between giving in and negotiating. This is analogous to the distinction between competition and cooperation. In competitive relationships, our pleasure comes from another person's loss. In cooperation, joy comes from working with the other person so that both can win. Competition is aggressive; cooperation is assertive. This is especially true, of course, in close relationships where competition is based on a lack of trust and cooperation is based on trying to make the relationship work. Blaming is competitive, for instance, because it is I who has to be right and you who must be wrong. The opposite is cooperation: "It doesn't matter who is right or wrong; let's work together to solve our problem."

Relationships that are competitive revolve around distance rather than intimacy. Each of us has a whole panoply of modes for keeping ourselves distant from others: competition, excellence, one-up-manship, running, judgments, secrets, intellectualizing, being right, being super anything. The choice to be separate is not aggressive in itself. It becomes aggressive when we pursue it as a secret agenda of our own while our partner believes we are committed to intimacy and cooperation.

Some energy has been put into inventing sports that are noncompetitive. The tension and anxiety associated with competing can give way to the ease and exuberance of pulling together so that victory means everyone is here, side by side, rather than I am up and you are down. Winning then means completing the project of cooperation.

- IMPERATIVES

Assertive people are highly sensitive to others' rights and so will carefully learn how to respect their right to act—even to act wrongly. This is especially crucial in relationships between parents and children. Constant imperatives only serve to keep children helpless and ultimately they will rebel in ways that may hurt them. Assertive parents will set timely limits, make agreements about the limits and then consistently follow through. "Pick up your clothes." "Do your chores." These are nagging and aggressive remarks. "We have an agreement that you will pick up your clothes. I would like you to keep your agreement." This is the assertive declaring of a fact and asking for what you need.

- TRESPASSING ON OTHERS' RIGHTS

The aggressive person will trespass on others' rights in gross ways (physical violence, stealing, cheating, lying, etc.) or in the subtle ways seen above. This is where feedback from others helps so much. They may see these subtly aggressive styles of behavior before we do.

Here Is an Example of Each of the Three Responses:

Someone owes you money and you would like it back:
The *assertive* person says, "You owe me five dollars; I'd like it back." She states her wish simply without reproach or reluctance.

The *nonassertive* person does not say anything. She fears asking for the money back, rationalizing: "It's not polite to ask for money back; it sounds selfish. It's better to wait until he decides to return it." She has handed her power over to her debtor.

The *actively aggressive* person might say, "What kind of welcher are you? You know you owe me five dollars; pay up."
The *passively aggressive* person might not say anything to the debtor but goes to all his friends and says, "He's dishonest. He doesn't pay back what he owes." Aggression often masks the fear of grief. "If I lose, I will have to feel sad. To avoid that pain, I will lash out and bully him into giving me what I want!" I am feeling the panic of having to grieve if I am cheated or if I lose out. This makes me insistent and persistent.

Assertive responses are usually indicative ("I want," "I am," "I will not"). Nonassertive responses are usually subjunctive ("If only," "He might"). Aggressive responses are often imperatives ("Do not," "Change this").

As you learn to be assertive, you will realize that your assertiveness is apparent not just in what you say, but in how you say it; in fact, what you say is quite secondary. These are the nonverbal clues that you have power:
Eye contact: Look at a person directly, rather than looking away.
Gestures: The same part of the brain that has to do with verbalizing has to do with gesturing. Use them freely and expressively.
Posture : Do not keep your head down or turned aside. Project posture that has a sense of power in it.

Voice inflection: Speak loudly enough so that you can be heard.

The very last on the list is the *words* that you speak. This is why role-playing assertive situations with a group or a friend who can give you feedback on your forcefulness is useful in building assertiveness.

Assertiveness is the life-style of the healthy ego.

Aggression is the life-style of the inflated, arrogant ego.

Passivity is the life-style of the impoverished ego.

OUR RIGHTS TO FEARLESSNESS

• You Have a Right to Ask.

You have a right to ask for 100% of what you want 100% of the time from 100% of the people. Do not ask for what you think is available or what you think you can obtain but ask for all that you want. Then negotiate.

• You Have the Right to Declare Your Rights.

"I resent your telling me I can't call you to ask you when you will complete this job. I have a right to call you and ask about the progress of our contract." Or: "You ask too many questions," a boss says. "I have a right to ask questions so that I can get things clear for myself."

• You Have a Right to Give No Excuses for What You Do, What You Have Done, or What You Will Do.

When someone invites you to a party, you do not have to say, "I can't come because I'm going to a meeting that night." You can simply say, "No, thank you." You have a right not to give a reason, but you may choose to give one in order to be sensitive to a friend.

• YOU HAVE THE RIGHT TO DECIDE TO WHAT EXTENT YOU WILL BE RESPONSIBLE FOR OTHER PEOPLE'S PROBLEMS.

"You have to pick me up because I do not have a car. You're my only way of getting there." You are not responsible for other people's predicaments, unless you choose to be, or unless that is the agreement. All expectations have to be based on agreements to be valid. The fact that something is necessary, convenient, habitual, or logical does not mean it has to be done by you.

• YOU HAVE A RIGHT TO CHANGE YOUR MIND.

"I know I agreed to car pool with you, but it has become more and more difficult for me, so I will not be continuing after this month. This gives you time to make new arrangements."

• YOU HAVE THE RIGHT TO MAKE MISTAKES.

"You're a nurse; you shouldn't make these mistakes." "Yes, I'm a nurse, but I'm also a human being, and I do make errors. I take responsibility for what I did." It is important to be responsible when exercising this right and the preceding one. Otherwise, these rights would be one-sided and cop-outs. The assertive person enjoys his rights while at the same time he acts them out with sensitivity to the rights of others.

• YOU HAVE A RIGHT TO BE ILLOGICAL IN YOUR DECISIONS.

When people say, "You can't do that; it's illogical," you can say, "Yes, I can. I see more in this than you may be seeing." When we have a sense of our own power, we do what we want to do without fear, and without letting ourselves be intimidated.

• YOU HAVE A RIGHT TO ACT IN YOUR OWN BEST INTERESTS.

"I was here before this man and want to be waited on first." Most of us are embarrassed to say things like that. "It sounds petty," or "greedy," etc. Underneath that inner self-criticism lies another message: "Do not be assertive; do not have any power; let other people have power over you; do not be yourself. Do not BE at all!"

- YOU HAVE A RIGHT TO BE NON-ASSERTIVE.

Assertiveness is always a matter of choice. Even after we have learned the skill of assertiveness, we can always choose to be non-assertive. You are in a theater. There are many empty seats. The men behind you are rowdy and rough. You can assertively speak up and ask them to quiet down. This will probably not work; so you simply change your seat. This is a legitimate choice of safety over assertiveness! Note that we are not acting in a vacuum; we are respecting time, space, and conditions.

- YOU HAVE A RIGHT TO BE SUPPORTED IN THE LIFESTYLE YOU CHOOSE.

This includes being an introvert in this extraverted world! This right requires that you look for the people who will be supportive of you. The assertive person is aware of the need for support in problem-solving, sexual and gender issues, processing of feelings, and decision-making. He seeks this support, knowing he has an inalienable right to pursue his own happiness in his own way. He/she works for laws that honor this.

ROADBLOCKS TO REAL COURAGE

Our life history gets in the way of courageous assertiveness: learning not to ask for what you want, not to take care of yourself, not to have power. In childhood we may have been taught to think that the recognitions, appreciations, and compliments that we needed were scarce, not enough to go around. "I'd better not ask for too much; there will not be any left." Or, "I'd better not give too much; I might not have any left."

These are the injunctions that may have led to our belief in scarcity:

- DON'T ASK FOR WHAT YOU WANT.

"If you're at someone's house, and you see some cookies you want, don't ask for them. If they're offered to you, say no. If they're offered a second time, you may say yes, but take only one." That is the recipe for politeness, for not getting any cookies, and for not being assertive. We change these don'ts to do's in assertiveness.

A second part of this is not asking for something, especially for emotional goods, because: "If you have to ask for it, it isn't worth it." What you are really saying here is that when something emerges from your own power, it has less value. If I ask you for twenty dollars or if you give me twenty dollars voluntarily, it is still twenty dollars. We don't use this reasoning with emotional values. We say, "I want you to instigate it," which means, "I want to wait until you become sensitive enough to know what I need." In all of this, we are like someone lying under a pear tree with his mouth open, waiting for a pear to fall in, instead of just reaching up and taking one.

- DON'T OFFER COMPLIMENTS TO OTHER PEOPLE.

They might suspect you: "What is he really after?" Not showing appreciation and not appreciating are behaviors inculcated in us early in life. The pay-off here is distance. Most of us fear intimacy. By not offering appreciations to others, we are keeping ourselves at arm's length from them. Thus no intimacy or commitment will be required of us.

- DON'T ACCEPT KINDNESS.

"*This* is a nice dress? I like yours better." We push compliments away, having been taught early in life to distrust kindness: "It may have a catch." We are quite unlike the cat who lets herself be stroked. She does not move away from strokes, or say, "Go pet the dog." She lets the strokes come into her body. She enjoys them. She knows she deserves them. A pay-off for not accepting love is never feeling obliged, eschewing ties. I will not owe you anything if I do not accept what you give me. This is another flight of the ego from intimacy.

- DON'T REJECT WHAT YOU DON'T WANT.

"If you are at Grandma's and she gives you something to eat that you don't like, eat it anyway. Don't say no; you might hurt her feelings." This means you do not have a right to reject what you do not want! This may result in resentment toward those who give you what they think you need. Some people may try to force something, or themselves, on you. Such harassment will go unchecked if you do not believe you have the right to say no to what you do not want or welcome.

- DON'T GIVE YOURSELF COMPLIMENTS.

"Don't toot your own horn." "Don't boast." "Don't brag." Why not? "I finally learned how to do a tune up, and I've saved so much money. I have more talent than I thought I did." This is legitimate self-valuing, moving from the fear base to the power base. Some might still call this arrogance. Can we say no to them?

Obstacles to the reclaiming of personal power flow from the tenets of the Protestant Ethic, which may have characterized our public school or religious background:

- Individual achievement through effort: "Everyone can be President." (Don't be your ordinary self.)

- Gratification is a consequence of performance, not an end in itself. (Don't enjoy.)

- Intelligence, not feeling, leads to truth. "Don't get emotionally involved." (Don't feel.)

• It's always a weakness to seek help to get over things. (Don't try not to suffer.)

• Working on a steady basis at the same job means stability, no matter how much you dislike the work. (Don't change.)

• What you gain by wit or effort is entirely yours and need not be shared. (Don't give.)

• In dealing with others, it is better to be right than flexible. (Don't feel.)

• Succeed even if it kills you. (Don't live.)

Compare the above injunctions to this list of healthy discernment criteria:

1. You have the ability to perceive clearly and to decide freely, i.e., without emotional confusion, psychological stress, or cognitive bias. This means not being at the mercy of moods, whims, fears, addictions, logic, or coercion.

2. Your desire, goal, plan, or decision has historical continuity in your life, i.e., it has stood the test of time. In particular, in the month(s) prior to making the choice, you have wanted it every day consecutively.

3. You are engaging in dialogue with the significant people in your life, with those who may be affected by your decision, with those who have any technical knowledge about your plan, with those who have made the same choice, with those who decided against making this choice, and with a therapist or support group, if appropriate.

4. You have the skills or talents required to carry out this task or you are taking the steps required to achieve it. (Vocation happens where bliss meets talent.)

5. You are committed to the goal strongly enough to see it through to its conclusion, no matter what challenges or hazards it might entail.

6. Your decision is conscientious, i.e., it requires no immoral activity or violation of others' rights to implement it. It is based on both love and self-esteem, not on aggression, ego, or self-depreciation.

7. There always remains one element of doubt in your mind. Absolute certainty may be a signal of a willful ego that refuses to explore creative alternatives or that dismisses possibilities before fully investigating them. Jung reminds us, "Certitude never led to discovery."

8. You have been noticing an inner confirmation of your choice through dreams, intuitions, and synchronicity (meaningful coincidence).

9. You have been receiving graces that confirm your choice, e.g., things falling into place automatically for you, access to powers and realizations that exceed the usual limits of your will and intellect, results that exceed effort. This is the wind-horse again, the successful interplay of effort and grace, of steps that are followed by shifts. Assisting forces seem to favor and forward your process. Afflicting forces are unable to daunt you, though they do inform you.

10. You are following your bliss. You have a self-confirming conviction of the rightness of this choice for you. You have an abiding, intuitive and bodily sense of pur-

pose. And finally, all of this results in deep serenity.

A creative soul emerges which is produced by the con-stellated archetype and possesses that compelling author-ity, not unjustly characterized as the voice of God. The nature of the soul is in accord with the deepest founda-tions of the personality as well as with its wholeness. It embraces conscious and unconscious and therefore tran-scends ego.
—Jung, "A Psychological View of Conscience"

WHEN FEAR MEETS SAFETY

At the beginning of this book, we saw that fears will always be in us, but that we can live with them, feel them safely, and act over them. The courage in assertiveness empowers us to face the world and conflicts safely. It does this by increasing our skills in expressing feelings openly and nonviolently. It teaches us how to be persistent, yet still open to negotiating for what we want. It frees us from the manipu-lations of unfair criticisms, blaming, and other power plays.

Being controlled is a matter of choice. A nonassertive lifestyle is something we are responsible for. Our parents and society may have headed us in that direction, but we stayed on course. Assertiveness helps us to see the course we have chosen. We were handed oppressive scripts, yet we can oper-ate "with our eyes open." There are percentages in responsi-bility but the largest percentage now is with us as adults.

Finally, assertiveness teaches us the consequences of aggression: isolation from relationship and intimacy. When we compete in relationships, we grow at another's expense. We put others down and gain a false sense of superiority. Assertiveness builds self-esteem and serenity so that our relationships become clearer, more intimate, and more per-sonally confirming.

There are no mistakes or failures in assertiveness while

we are practicing these skills. If we find that we do not assert ourselves in an area we have practiced (in role play with a friend or group), we have not failed but only discovered that we need to begin a step or two lower in the hierarchy of practice. Once we find our level of safety (the level at which we are successful), we build our assertive skills more exponentially.

We have seen that assertiveness is "truth." The truth is that you do want things, and the truth is that you have a right to ask for them. The truth is whatever you are gaining clarity about. The truth is taking responsibility for what you are today and what you have done; what you did yesterday and what you are going to do tomorrow.

Sometimes in an assertive interaction, you may find out something painful from a partner. So, *today you have the pain and the truth; tomorrow you have only the truth,* and that remains forever as a frontispiece for new volumes of lively energy and freedom from the grip of fear. (Ultimately, as we saw above, fear has no real power to grip us, only the storylines of powerlessness that surround it do.) Rilke describes the perfect relationship as one "where two liberties meet, embrace, salute, and protect each other." It is not throwing one's liberty away; it is cherishing yours and someone else's. "We can do nothing against the truth, but only for it," says St. Paul.

Occasionally, we find great courage and suddenly act heroically. This may not be the power of the ego. It may be the Self that reaches out to a helpless person in distress by inciting courage in an ordinary passerby or witness. Not I but a Higher Power than I intervened to save you by encouraging me for you. This is what St. Francis meant by becoming an instrument of peace.

7.

The Spiritual Path to Fearlessness

BEYOND "TO DO" INTO "TO BE"

If I had two loaves of bread,
I would sell one for hyacinths
For they would feed my soul.
—Arabic Saying

If I go to the pear tree for a pear, I am taking care of myself by actively nourishing my body. If I sit under the tree and gaze at the last flowers of the garden, I am taking care of a deeper need: the need to respond to beauty. I am not giving up pears, but I am more richly expanding my experience of the universe by allowing myself to appreciate more of it. I am allowing myself to be present for whatever may next surprise me. This is the receptive mode of consciousness that balances the assertive mode. It is the gateway to grace, the complement of effort.

Handling fear takes more than acting bravely. As spiritual receptiveness grows, we realize more and more that we are deeply involved with our world. Our awareness now becomes the very object of change, not the means to it. We are changing because we appreciate our connectedness. This is where happening completes doing. It is the other side of the assertive style that uses new awarenesses as the means for reaching goals.

Once we trust our universe, we lighten up (enlightenment). We drop our need to change our nightmares to good dreams. We simply wake up. We drop all ego identifications that kept us rigidly bound to goals and success. Since we have expanded our awareness of our "self" to include everyone else, we are less protective of our ego. Now we feel the inner protectedness of the human community. We ask less, "What is my goal?" and more, "What is my destiny?"

Our self becomes an existential axis of awareness that at once observes and transcends our actions. We awaken then to all the possibilities that exist beyond our immediate awareness. We tune in on the amusing aspects of our experience.

The self that observes and transcends appreciates the truth of something so thoroughly that it goes through and beyond it. We become immanent to events, experiencing them from within. This is a departure from the dualistic world of subject and object, knower and known. We go beyond our personal boundaries and even the boundaries of time and space.

You do this every time you let yourself experience a fear fully. You enter your fear, not as something you know (object), but as if you were at the very heart of it (subject). Boundaries that protected you in the past become insignificant. You open every scary door into your own emotional mansion. You are happy to notice that you go on existing. You abide throughout the fear and then pass beyond its pale. The self that entered the fear and the self that emerged are you, but the latter you is a renewed, recapitulated, more courageous self. Struggling against fear reinforces it.

Paradoxically, we go beyond by going within. When we live at the razor's edge of a painful emotion, we are cut by it. When we enter the core of our experience and stay there, it reveals itself to us as transitory, not so truculent after all, not as overwhelming as we had feared. How long do we stay? Until one of us disappears, the fear or the self. And it will always be the fear.

By going beyond the limits we have set for—or rather against—ourselves, we gain the full range of emotion, surrender to our personal moment, and abide undefended and resourceful. The "I" that then remains is the I that is one with the universe: both immanent and transcendent.

Handling fear involves articulating our truth and acting in fearless ways. Assertiveness, a specific program for handling fear, progresses from clarity to asking for what we want to taking responsibility for ourselves. The phases of spiritual receptiveness are less well-defined. We move from self-awareness to letting go to self-transcendence and compassion. Self-awareness coincides with clarity; letting go corresponds to asking for what we want; and self-transcendence, with its attendant compassion, corresponds to taking responsibility. These are the dimensions of handling fear with higher consciousness. This is how a goal for oneself becomes a destiny for the world.

We become aware of the intuitions that influence our choices. We find ourselves more able to take cues from our body in an effortless way. We notice a decrease in the gap between experience and awareness. This means that we are taking responsibility for our experience. Taking action follows effortlessly as the horse follows the urgings of the wind.

Awareness—active looking within—means seeing nothing separate inside myself; thus, pure awareness is nothing objective. It is pure Subject since there is only one of us anywhere and already. This is referred to as the Transpersonal Self. The perceiver is one with the universe that he perceives, so that the objective universe, as well as my subjective self, disappears into the act of pure non-dual seeing. This means that *fear only finds its exit when the ego is on its way out.*

As we are transformed, we move from analytic thinking to integrative thinking. We synthesize attachment and detachment. We finally heal what before seemed irreconcilable difference, that is, the desire to be intimate with the world and yet far enough away from its distractions to remain centered.

Secondly, as we live beyond ego, we find that our actions

are fewer and more significant. Nonattachment to outcomes means more responsible actions since actions are responsive to reality, not to wishes.

Finally, in a transpersonal perspective, everything about our predicament is perfect. We honor where we are and the moment we are in. We combine change and self-acceptance in a natural, present-respecting rhythm. We are "still and still moving," as T.S. Eliot says.

Being in this enlightened place is not difficult. What is difficult is missing it. So much of our energy goes into sabotaging the enduring moment of recognition that what we are and have is perfect enough. This is why there is nothing to do: we already are centered. We lose track of this fact by remaining in our heads. As we open, we become aware of how much truth is accessible to us by effortlessly tuning in on what is.

Jung said, "The approach to the numinous is the real therapy. And inasmuch as you attain to the numinous experience, you are released from the curse of pathology." The accent is not on what needs to be done but on the urgent movement in our personal history that takes us closer and closer to the luminous center of the universe, which is the center in ourselves. We are ourselves the paradigm, the hologram of the universe. Therapy is simply our locomotion from awareness of oneness (samadhi) to perception without clinging or judging (satori). The transition is simply seeing what is here now. This is the opposite of the dualism that wants to get something from what we see or judge what we see.

As we approach the numinous, the illuminated center in ourselves where we are one with all, we discover that real seeing is recognition of each reality as a hologram of all reality. Julian of Norwich, the 14th century English mystic, saw a hazelnut in her palm and realized in an enlightened moment that this was the universe. "We have ever more perfect eyes in a world in which there is always more to see," writes Teilhard de Chardin. Even western scientists state that the left brain is inadequate for creative thinking. Einstein once stated, "My intellect was of no help in discovering the fundamental laws." He learned these by intuition. The French philosopher Henri Bergson adds, "The mind is naturally unable to grasp the truth."

SPIRITUAL RECEPTIVENESS

Spiritual receptiveness is a skill of nondoing. It can be an epilogue or adjunct to assertiveness, a balance and complement to assertiveness. Assertiveness is learned by practice. Spiritual receptiveness *happens* when choices are made that support the Here and Now as the fundamental reality. Spiritual receptiveness is not abstract as much as elusive. This is why it can only be approximated, both verbally and actively.

We defined assertiveness in terms of personal empowerment. This is will as will power. Spiritual receptiveness balances this view by describing empowerment as willingness to accept the givens of existence and act in accord with one's personal experience as it unfolds. Assertiveness means actively working on reality to change it. Spiritual receptiveness means honoring reality and changing with it.

Receptiveness has to do with the release of the softer side of the self while still protecting one's integrity by balancing it with assertive behavior. Assertiveness posits and strengthens the self; spiritual receptiveness goes beyond it. This "going beyond" is the point of contact with "Power greater than oneself."

Spiritual receptiveness happens by meditation, affirmations, and other spiritual practices. "Letting go" is the main feature of this balance. Here are ten basic areas that relate to the surrender of the ego each of which brings you to an exponential dimension of spiritual change:

1. Letting go of limiting, rigid roles,

2. Letting go of the belief that I am entitled to be taken care of,

3. Letting go of attachment to outcomes so that a balance occurs between making things happen (effort) and allowing things to happen (effortlessness),

4. Letting go of the fear that others may know who we are or what our agenda is,

5. Letting go of the need to be right or in control, to be hard on ourselves and others,

6. Letting go of old resentments, blame, grudges, and the desire for vengeance,

7. Letting go of an "either. . .or" attitude,

8. Letting go of the need to cover up our feelings or to flee our upheavals instead of cooperating with them so that new vistas appear,

9. Letting go of disowning the parts of ourselves that scare, shame, or excite us,

10. Letting go of the fear of intimacy, aloneness, change, loss, and of our own potential.

We often act because of inner and even unconscious shoulds and injunctions, as noted above. They are the vocabulary of the inner accusatory voice we continually hear and react to. As we become more self-aware, we perceive our shoulds more vividly. They appear to us as inner self-abdications, reflections of early training in self-denial and self-annihilation. In a way, we make the superego conscious, catching it red-handed. The realm of choice is then expanded.

We distinguish here the positive should that serves the

social order and fosters our personal freedom and the negative shoulds that serve the social order at the expense of our personal freedom. We drop the negative compulsive shoulds and change the positive shoulds to simple personally owned decisions.

As self-awareness grows in us, we no longer implicate others as the pain-causers (e.g., parents, society). We no longer seek to extricate ourselves from the pain. We simply get out of the way so that the pain can pass by. The strength in awareness is the strength to make friends with our pain rather than dodging it. Then the implication of our parents as the culprits who made us so inadequate loses its meaning. There is no blame, only accountability that may or may not ever be acknowledged by them. We are aware of our history and grieve it. We honor our history and are now more passionately involved in our own present.

It is at this point that effortlessness begins. We are no longer fighting shoulds or holding on to resentments. We let go. We cease inhibiting ourselves and cease being angry at those we blame for our own inhibitions. "There may be some state of mind in which one could continue without effort because nothing is required to be held back," says Virginia Woolf.

In our psychological work of handling fear assertively, the emphasis is on asking for what we want. As we become more receptive, we trust that we will always have what we need. Asking becomes less crucial to us; letting go takes precedence. This means dissociating ourselves from roles, scripts, and even relationships that limit us. As long as we are attached to a certain definition of ourselves, we are holding ourselves back from a rich variety of experiences. As we drop limiting identifications, we allow ourselves room to respond to the existential moments that present themselves to us one-by-one. This is what is meant by living in the here and now. It involves a definite shift away from our dependence on tried-and-true methods of operating in the world. Instead we discover a new realm of options that goes beyond our old self-image.

A dramatic example of this occurs in the *Odyssey* when Ulysses, after leaving the island of Calypso, is shipwrecked. He has lost his crew and fleet and is alone in the sea holding onto a single plank. Hope seems lost when suddenly Leucothea, a sea goddess, appears and tells him that the only way to survive is to let go. His logical mind tells him that the tried-and-true method of maintaining flotation is in holding onto the plank. Yet his intuition, represented by the goddess, tells him to let go of it and thus invent a new and bold response to his here and now crisis. He chooses (as he does throughout the Odyssey) to listen to the female part of himself and to trust audacious intuition. He lets go of the plank and more: his garments. He treads water without physical supports. Then the goddess gives him a magical push that propels him effortlessly to his next destination. Notice two features of the story that are significant: Ulysses had just left the arms of Calypso, rejecting her offer of divinity and preferring to return to his wife, Penelope. He chose not to be allured by the temptation of a quick and easy advance in consciousness but rather to continue his journey home gradually. This was the first choice he made that prepared him for the miraculous rescue to follow. His second preparation for empowerment was his hopelessness. No intuitions came to him while he was safe at sea. Marvels occur when there is room for them. This theme of "having nothing left" recurs often in spiritual literature as the precursor to enlightenment.

William James notes that the conversion experience is always preceded by depression. The "we had hoped" of the two disciples en route to Emmaus was the preface to their enlightenment. In the final disappointment, when all expectations are dropped, the Everything breaks bread with us.

Ulysses dropped his role as seafarer, as he had already dropped his relationship with the seductive Calypso, both limiting roles. We move spiritually as we drop attachment to who we think we are. To ask is to know your identity; to let go is to transcend it. "I drop the roles and identifications I have collected and live from the authentic center of myself." "I am still a loving person when I let go of the need to make things come out right for others."

Notice that in these affirmations and indeed in this entire transpersonal dimension of experience, what matters is the changing of our attachments to identifications and outcomes. You may put effort into a project of change or care about the outcome of an event, but drop the belief that you are the doer and that everything depends upon your effort or that the "wrong" outcome will devastate you. This is not stoicism, planned nonconcern or choice not to care. T.S. Eliot prays to Mary: "Teach us to care and not to care." We cease trying to control everything. Our predicament is honorable as it is. As we drop ego involvement, we meet a new "I" in each dynamic moment. Things no longer matter because there is no solid I to have them, no need for security from them. The truth becomes more valuable to us than our wishes.

As we transcend ourselves, we move from dualism to playfulness with opposites. We drop "either...or" and are comfortable with "both...and." As we let go of the need to possess others and to demand our own way in relationships, we move from rigidity to resilience, from demand to acceptance: "I can both remain in this relationship and accept you as you are." This is seeing the space, hearing the silence, finding the poetry of spiritual freedom.

The transformation attendant upon self-transcendence is a progression from passion to compassion. Our passion for keeping things our way yields to a consciousness of others. It is a movement away from the ego that is contained to the self that is connected. This latter self is so intimately bound up with other beings that multiplicity disappears into oneness. This oneness was manifested in the great mystics who found their love of nature and their sense of service growing in proportion to their experience of enlightenment. On Mount Tabor, when

Peter asked to hold on to the moment of enlightenment—" Let us build three tabernacles..."—he was soon reminded of the needs of others at the foot of the mountain.

As we become more open to the fact of our oneness with the universe, passion gives way to a rich sense of completion. We always and already are and have all that can be sought. Notice how ancient Greek plays end on a note of repose, as do the plays of Shakespeare. The passions have been played out and now the audience can breathe easily. This is the same repose experienced by those who have gone beyond their own ego needs and awakened to the feelings of others and to the sighs of the universe.

There is a sense of amity and an end to grudge in self-transcendence. Going beyond ego means that vengeance and the desire to punish disappear. We are not holding anything against anyone. We are simply holding everyone and letting ourselves be held. A nonviolent love emerges where before there was hurt and anger. A striking example of this appeared in the drawing of a child with cancer. In the interests of self-healing, he visualized the cancer cells as goblins attacking him from an aircraft. He drew himself shooting down the goblins, as a way of ridding himself of the noxious cells. But on each falling goblin, he drew a parachute. The evil of his illness did not supplant his inner loving kindness.

Enlightenment ultimately means lightening up, not letting things become heavy, not letting any experience or series of experiences assume the aspect of the absolute. Enlightenment means no longer being in the power of any person or event. It is the realization that we decide to let things affect us either painfully or humorously, either heavily or barely.

We let go of our need to impose upon events an ego-aggrandizing significance or upon others a judgment that diminishes them. Events become personal to us as they are, not as arrows against us or accolades for us. We simply own and honor events. When enlightenment occurs, when we finally let ourselves see what has been there all the time, we return to our ordinary life, but find it all shimmering and sacred as the mythical heroes did upon their return from the underworld.

Enlightenment is not a prize at the end of a race or search but finally being present in the world as it is. As long as we are looking for something from the world, we never really see it, as the pickpocket does not see the wizard, but only his pockets! We reclaim the world and the moment as ours whenever we drop the desire to make things come out our way and simply let things happen, trusting that every way is our way. We remind ourselves of what Govinda said, "The certainty that nothing can happen to us that does not in our innermost being belong to us is the foundation of fearlessness."

In a Hasidic story, a rabbi dreams there is a treasure buried under a certain bridge. He then travels the countryside and eventually finds the bridge. With great alacrity, he climbs down under the bridge and digs. But though he digs and digs, he finds nothing. The rabbi then sits dejectedly on a stone. A hobo asks him why he looks so sad. The rabbi tells him of the dream and the fruitless search. "Funny," says the hobo. "I dreamed of a treasure buried under the hearth in a rabbi's house, and he looked a lot like you!" The rabbi hurried home and, of course, dug up a great treasure.

Besides the reference to enlightenment ensuing upon disappointment, notice the other momentous truth here: all that we need is here, but it seems we still have to make that long journey out and hear from others far from home that all is within.

Someone cannot be enlightened. *Only no one is enlightened.* As long as I am a subject doing this to get enlightenment, I am disqualifying myself from it. Strike one is believing I am a separate subject and doer, strike two is believing a method is all that works, and strike three is attachment to the desire to become enlightened. All we can do is nothing. All we can be open to is everything. The shift to spiritual receptiveness is precisely that: putting ourselves in the best position for enlightenment to happen.

It is the last trick of the ego that its action is so powerful that it can sabotage our growth or our experience of enlightenment. Actually, the ego cannot do that, try as it may. The Self is revealed when the timing is right. It emerges on its own, irrespective of our efforts to evoke or subdue it. Again, since there is no doer, there is no saboteur! Do not give your ego so much credit! In the final analysis, it is only a bystander in the event of enlightenment and transformation, an event that occurs in a realm beyond ego altogether.

Transformation happens through the awareness of oneness, not through struggle. When you fight to gain control over yourself, you have already lost. Nonresistance to our passions and feelings without the need to do anything is the path to awareness, awareness of the absolute oneness beyond duality.

Whenever we try to do something about our fears, including thinking about them, we are only reinforcing them. We are the police riding to raid a casino with the sirens on. Moving to the effortless intuitive mode, we let ourselves experience our tensions fully. We remain present for them and so pass through and beyond them. We stay with the tension as a bamboo leaf lets itself be heaped with falling snow. The heavier the weight (tension), the closer the moment of dropping it. *We stay with what is, and it changes; we stay with who we are, and we change.*

Struggle leads to winning or losing which then reinforces the ego. This furthers the illusion that the ego exists as a solid mass which requires occasional or constant inflation. Our intuition tells us there is only one of us, and that one exists beyond the pale of victory or loss. *When I give up trying to be a Master, I am no longer a slave.* In other words, what I do not do still happens. Sexually, I am receptive whenever I transcend the joke/belief that everything depends on what I do or how I perform. I pass beyond the role of actor and doer and simply remain present as everything that needs to happen happens.

This is the same mystical sense that athletes (especially runners) have when they combine tension and exhilaration, anxiety and joy. The fusion of these apparent opposites makes sports another paradigm for the enlightened state. Niels Bohr's principle of complementarity appears here: opposites are not separate but cohere and combine.

Our life partakes of this same integration when doer and act become doing, when mastery becomes letting go. This is all a cosmic joke that makes us laugh (once we understand it). It is the same mindful laugh that we might express when we realize that an onion is only layer after layer with no solid core at all. Making that same discovery about the self frees us and then we become less goal-and effort-oriented. The less we see ourselves as separate and solid, the more we let ourselves trust the graces everywhere available to us.

The result of this transformation is freedom from fear. You have befriended your fears so entirely that you no longer fear so desperately. The ego vanishes now, preferences vanish, questions vanish, attachments vanish, that vague feeling of incompletion vanishes, apprehension about performance or adequacy vanishes, obscure feelings of guilt about pleasure vanish: you have put your ego away.

You go beyond your mind! You take leave of the linear thinking and worrying about what may happen and let your mind become open to its own power of intuition and synthesis. Now you see beyond your neediness. You see the world not from a fear base but from your center of open awareness where nothing can ever go wrong.

Freedom is the ability to experience a circumstance without projecting an ego over or against it. Free, lively energy moves uninhibitedly with the rhythms that your body shows you from within. It does not arrest its flow, nor try to create desire or get the desirable. It no longer reaches into the moving stream to capture the bright pebble but enters the stream and moves with its flow. This is the ease that comes when we no longer poke but stroke. It is playful indulgence.

Jesus says: "The wind blows where it will and you do not know where it goes or from whence it came." You enter the rhythms of personal change and the vicissitudes of interests. You follow an inner motion which now leads you to frequent activity, now to less, now to none. You are hearing the chimes of your own inner clock.

This is entering shunyata, the Eastern notion of emptiness: there is nothing to be held on to or held to; there is no one to do the holding. We are released from the habitual tension that comes from the necessity to do and to grasp. Emptiness here means not rushing into the environment to have needs met. It is the enlightened serenity that comes with trust that without having to do anything, all that you need will come to you. It is the spiritually chosen void.

Freedom from attachment to effort is like a Zen koan in which you pass beyond the polar alternatives of assertion and denial by confronting and acknowledging the impasse with a laugh. This is what Alice did when she suddenly gave up trying to make the Queen's court follow sane logical rules. "You are nothing but a pack of cards," she said. Thus was she at once released from the need to do anything at all to make things come out right. She surrendered to the inner comedy of the moment and so cut through it. The word surrender here means letting go of the belief that you can do it all and even that you are a doer at all. Surrender does not mean giving up as in a military defeat, but rather dropping the illusion that all of what happens to you depends on you.

The central issue in both psychological work and spiritual practice is the integration of the self through the perfect fusion of power and intimacy. This is a path as well as a skill. No one of us is clear all the time, or asks for what he or she wants all the time, or takes responsibility for feelings and actions all the time. We are all always operating within a spectrum. We are always in process. Sometimes we let go; sometimes we go beyond our egos, sometimes not.

Psychological growth is never about quantity or even achievement. "I acted assertively 100 times today." "I imaged perfectly today" would not be as sanguine for us as "I sense that I'm progressing, however haltingly, in integrating my needs for power and my ability to let go. It's all coming together." This is the move toward oneness and away from interruption, polarity, distance, and the desire for victory. It is the harmonious music of the spheres become resonant in us.

Saint Simeon the Younger said, "I saw Him in my house. Among all the everyday things He appeared unexpectedly and became utterly united and merged with me, and leaped over to me without anything in between, as fire to iron, as light to glass. And He made me like fire and like light. And I became that which I saw before and beheld from afar. I do not know how to relate this miracle to you. I am man by nature, and God by grace." The two—the hero and his ultimate god, the seeker and the found—are thus understood as the outside and inside of a single, self-mirrored mystery, which is identical with the mystery of the manifest world. The great deed of the supreme hero is to come to the knowledge of this unity in multiplicity and then to make it known.

—Joseph Campbell

8.

Affirming Fearlessness

Something inside us wants to bloom: it requires cultivation by us, energy from the universe, and an inner urgency all its own that wants to live and grow. We expend effort to cultivate our potential; we are open to receive the graces of the universe, and we trust an inner zeal for evolution that makes us want to live and grow.

Affirmations work in all three of these areas. We do the work of designing, remembering, and using them. Powers beyond our own making then come to aid us. Every affirmation is another way of saying yes to our inner yearning to live fully.

To Do: Affirmations

Designing your own affirmations is an important part of the process of letting go of fear and moving along on our journey toward wholeness. An affirmation is a positive declaration of what is already true in the unconscious and now is ready to be manifested in conscious life. The first step is to hearken to our own inner world to find out what wants to emerge into the light of consciousness. To do this, look at your dreams, your intuitions, any meaningful coincidences that have been happening, any images that keep coming back to you or that hold your attention.

All of these come from your inner unconscious self and defy rational definition. Try this exercise: focus on an image that has held your fascination all your life and establish a dialogue with it, asking it what it has always wanted to tell you. Close your eyes and focus in on it as if it were within you, and listen to what it may say. Just a word or phrase is enough. Then respond. See how long the dialogue can last. If you prefer, do this all in writing or music or by movement or in any creative way you choose. Let the image speak to you in whatever mode you are comfortable with. Be receptive; do not dictate to it or change it to tame it or tone it down.

Now design a positive statement that summarizes the results of your imaging. Make it present tense, first person singular, not a wish but a declaration, not using "I can" but "I am" or "I do" or "I allow" or "I honor."

You are designing a personal yes to an image that has held your attention. It has done this because it wants to help you in moving on toward higher self-esteem and toward your special individual destiny. Its meaning is your meaning.

An affirmation brings your reluctant conscious into step with your ongoing unconscious evaluation. Remember your unconscious self is already whole and knows no past or future. Within you there is an eternal simultaneous now that is full of miraculous powers and unconditional love. Our destiny is to let our unique life story articulate this wonderful and healing wholeness in our daily world. An affirmation closes the gap between capacity (an inner plenitude) and performance (an external behavior).

Affirmations are ways of saying yes to the very best you can be, to the very best that you already are inside. These affirmations are oriented toward building your self-esteem. Self-esteem means valuing yourself as you really are. These affirmations also help you go beyond your own ego to spiritual transformation. Spirituality is the longing in us for a meaning that is not limited by time or place. Health in spirituality and personality unite to make us intuitive about which paths make most sense for us. When we integrate our personal and spiritual lives, we find ourselves becoming more and more passionate toward ourselves and others. An unconditional love for others emerges but never clashes with our own need to take care of ourselves. We can show sane love for others and still maintain the boundaries of love for ourselves. This is our destiny.

The affirmations that follow include, summarize, and expand the points made in the preceding chapters. The use of these affirmations will support you in putting assertiveness and spiritual receptiveness into practice to transcend fear and live in accord with your destiny.

Read all the affirmations and choose the ones that best describe what you want to be true of you. An affirmation stretches your consciousness. You affirm what has struck you because that is how you discover what your unconscious is ready to articulate into consciousness. You may alter the way an affirmation is stated here. You may come up with your own. The best one is the one you choose and revise if necessary. Write that one out, and repeat it throughout the day. Some affirmations listed here you will not even notice until exactly the time you are ready for them. Each one is meant to take you beyond where you are now.

It is helpful to read your list aloud each day for at least ten minutes. Repeat them often throughout the day. The repetition and the remembering install self-esteem into your consciousness. Pay attention to the affirmations that challenge you most. They help you advance to your next step. Gradually you concentrate on exactly the ones you need most. To be drawn to any one of them means readiness to put it into practice. The affirmations below do not follow a specific order, so beginning and ending at any point is appropriate.

From a place of calm abiding, form an image of yourself as having the quality the affirmation depicts. Affirmations are suggestions to your inner mind, and it is best not to apply rational thought processes to them. Let them flow through without question, as friends who enter your house without being asked to show their identification.

Acknowledge that the "I" of each affirmation refers to you and that each of these affirmations describes you as you truly are—though your present behavior and rational mindset may tell you otherwise. Gradually, you will notice better feelings about yourself, clearer choices as you face new issues, and a deepening serenity.

Each next affirmation will have to do with the transition you are about to initiate, or have just completed, or are in the midst of. Affirmations help us move; they commit us to going on. Plot yourself now with respect to a transition (beginning, middle, end) and state your status with an affirmation. Remember that whether you are in the middle, late or past stage, your affirmation is always in the present. Here are examples using one specific life transition issue:

- I let go of my fear of losing my grown children.

- I am happy to see my children move on.

- I parent myself by using my free time more nurturantly.

- I grieve the departure of my children and let go of them.

- I get on with my life.

- I keep finding new energies in myself.

Your inner self keeps giving you messages and clues about which steps to take next. Jung says "attention to the unconscious pays it a compliment that guarantees its cooperation." The psyche and the universe collaborate so that events occur and people enter our lives just at the times we are ready to learn something or to take our next step. Intuition, therapy, feedback from supportive friends, and our own power of imaging help de-code these messages so that we can move from information to affirmation.

Once we begin using an affirmation, our bluff is called. Choices arise that test its mettle. Do we really mean it? If we affirm, "I let go more and more," perhaps losses will come our way since our unconscious has been instructed that we are ready to let go. An affirmation like, "I seek and embrace new challenges," may lead to new opportunities arising from unusual sources. We have to mean business when we use affirmations. They really work!

As you say yes to the events and choices, you support the sincerity of your resolve. You then become more receptive to your inner world. You will notice that you hear more from within. You are tuned in to your intuitive powers. Attention to the unconscious leads to more and more dialogue with it. When you stop listening, the inner voice becomes silent.

Gradually the choices lead to a change in your conscious behavior. Now there is no longer a gap between capacity and performance, between what is unconsciously true and what is consciously acted out. Now you can drop the affirmation. It has done its work of expanding you.

Usually a new one will arise that takes you to the next level of progress. You have taken the *steps*—through your series of yeses to the choices validating your affirmation—and now a *shift* occurs automatically. This is how effort and grace work together for you.

Do not use negatives such as "not" or "never." Do not use "can" or "could" or "will." The unconscious has no past or future or wish. It understands only here, now, is, am, and yes. Using more than one at a time is appropriate when they reflect one theme at a time.

Say them aloud and silently. Put them on tape and listen to them. Draw them, act them out, dance them, sing them. Write them on cards that you keep in every place you see often, e.g., your car, desk, bathroom, mirror, refrigerator, wallet, etc.

As often as possible, be sure to form an image of yourself displaying the newly affirmed behavior. As an exercise, do this sitting quietly for three minutes each day. Drop the affirmation if it does not work soon, i.e., within a month or less. You have then not located an appropriate affirmation for your level of readiness. Remember, "working" means you have begun to be presented with choices and challenges that speak directly to the subject of the affirmation, or you have put it into effect with practical behavioral change.

Tell your affirmation to friends whenever you think it appropriate.

Design instant once-only affirmations when specific stimuli arise. This makes double duty from your thoughts or behavior. For instance, as you remember to use your seatbelt, say "I take care of myself more and more." As you reject smoking, say "I care about my health more and more."

Here are some affirmations that help to expand consciousness and fearlessness:

I have a right to happiness.

I feel better and better about who I am.

I am doing more and more to grow up.

I show more love than ever.

I take responsibility for working on the things in me that are ready for change.

Every barrier is a threshold for me.

Grace meets me in every person.

Grace finds me in every challenge.

Grace visits me in every obstacle.

I am a channel of the light that consciousness brings.

I am strongly grounded in compassion for myself and others.

I keep tuning in to an abiding wholeness within me.

I accept my limitations and I transcend my limitations.

I let go of my need to control, judge, attack and expect.

I feel an unconditional, inalienable, and indestructible love within and around me.

I show my unconditional love in my every thought, word and deed.

I see through and smile at the rationalizations that fight to keep me tied to old habits and fears.

I let go of the pictures I carry of how I want things to be or the hope of how they could be.

I am always self-renewing.

I let go of the false self I learned to project out of fear.

My present conflicts are my work.

My present predicament is full of wisdom.

I am perfect; I am complete even when things are falling apart.

My inner inviolate wholeness lives through every chaos.

This, like every chaos, completes itself in peace.

I have ever-surprising powers of self-restoration.

I accept my losses in life and grieve them fully.

I allow every human feeling.

I ask for what I want.

I take responsibility for my thoughts, feelings and behavior.

I am already and always fully healthy in my relationships.

I let go of the need to force people to give me what I want.

I let go of any sense of entitlement.

I tell others what my limits are.

I tell others what my suspicions, doubts, and wishes are.

I tell others when and how I admire them, when and how I am afraid of them, when I and how I love them, when and how I am angry at them.

I show anger and love at the same time.

I show my fears and let go of the need to act them out.

I say no without guilt.

I always have choices in life.

I show others how vulnerable I am and thereby have power.

I let go of the belief that I am a victim in any way.

I continually notice and am thankful for the automatic shifts that keep happening within me.

I notice love coming my way from every direction, in every circumstance, at every moment.

I let go of the need to control and find real power.

I trust my intuitions.

I acknowledge what I strongly admire in others as something unowned in myself.

I acknowledge what I strongly despise in others as something unowned in myself.

I foster nurturant parental love within myself.

I watch out for the wounded, hurt child within.

I trust myself to receive love and to handle hurt.

I trust myself to receive loyalty and handle betrayal.

I admit my fears of abandonment and engulfment.

I let others get close, and I let others go.

I love myself and share this love in intimate relationships.

I look for the good and praise it.

I love to give and receive.

I accept others as they change, make choices, show me how different they are, and refuse to do things my way.

I tell my story and let go of my story.

I drop the need to be right, to hold back, to get even.

I make room for the gaps that open in my life.

I always know when to take hold and when to let go.

I drop the impulse to be hard on myself.

I allow margins of error.

I accept challenges while still feeling fear.

I honor my destiny to show in my lifetime the timeless love within me.

I bring the light of consciousness into my personal world.

I let the imperishable rose of wholeness bloom in me.

I carry the grail of wholeness to every barren land in my life and world.

I am an epiphany of wholeness.

I trust what happens without having to know why.

I trust the something new that keeps appearing.

I am love unconditionally flourishing in every human condition.

I am in the best place to show love.

I am facing things that release my love.

I am with people who teach me to love.

I choose to show love again and again in every way to everyone.

I maintain unconditional love *and* my boundaries.

I make spiritual choices and choices that honor love and self-esteem.

I welcome the changes of time.

I welcome my time to win

        to give in

        to have

        to let go

        to make my mark

        to dissolve

        to find a foothold

        to fall into a gap

        to fight

to surrender

to stay

to move on.

Now I see it all with love and amusement.

Now design a personal affirmation that fits an insight that has come recently. (Turn it into an affirmation.) Here is an example: you realize you fear closeness. "I acknowledge my fear of closeness and get closer."

Form an affirmation that reverses an old parental injunction; for example, you often heard in childhood, "You are lazy and will not amount to anything." Reverse that to, "I am industrious and enthusiastic about my work. My work nurtures me. My career makes me feel better and better about myself."

Another theme for affirmations is sexuality. Look at your sexual style and behavior. Design an affirmation that honors it and enhances it:

- My sexual style has integrity.

- I give and receive intimacy.

- I show my love through my sexuality.

- I honor my sexual choices.

- I honor my sexual orientation.

- I integrate sex and intimacy.

- My sexuality is healthier every day.

Find a relationship issue and use an affirmation together

with a partner. Write it together and use it together and separately:

- Our relationship is becoming healthier every day.

- I ask for what I want.

- I show love more deeply.

- I bring love everywhere I go.

- I find love everywhere I go.

- I allow my partner to get close.

- I allow my partner to have space.

- I give and receive intimate love.

- I keep agreements.

- I handle obstacles.

- I listen to my partner more and more.

- I hear his feelings and respond to them.

- I admit my neediness and my fears.

- I let go of the need to be combative.

Use affirmations also to befriend and integrate your shadow (the disowned part of us which we refuse to acknowledge). The positive shadow is the untapped potential that we project onto others as strong admiration. The negative shadow is the disavowed, unacceptable side of us that we project onto others as strong dislike.

Form affirmations to befriend the positive shadow by stating that you have the very characteristics you admire in others: "I am assertive and clear." "I am generous." "I am growing in self-esteem." "I am freed from the grip of fear." Design affirmations to befriend your negative shadow by stating that you have access to the lively positive counterpart of the negative unowned behavior within you. If you despise people who are controlling, say "I release my leadership ability." If you dislike lying in others, say "I am more and more imaginative." If the issue is arrogance, say "I am confident in myself."*

Use affirmations to rebuild broken areas of your psyche and spiritual life using the power of paradox. Paradox is the language of the unconscious. Since affirmations help turn unconscious processes into conscious choices, they work more efficaciously when stated as paradoxes. For example, if you have lost your faith and lament it, say "I have unshakable faith." Soon you will locate where your faith is still alive and where it can be reconstructed in new ways. If you feel ashamed of the past, say "I am proud of my life as it is."

Notice how in each of these you are reversing the evidence of your mind and senses. Spiritual wisdom is in precisely this dismantling of the ego's stranglehold on reality. If you believe you are losing your touch in your career, you might say the following affirmation: "I have talents beyond imagination." If you feel life is passing you by, "I am more and more keenly alive and lively." If you imagine hope is gone, "I have every reason for optimism."

The unconscious loves paradox, though your rational mind finds it contradictory. The more paradoxical an affirmation, the better. Defy logic to release your healing powers:

---

*See the chapter in my book on befriending the shadow for a list of other characteristics and their lively counterparts: *How to Be an Adult: A Handbook on Psychological and Spiritual Integration*, Paulist Press, 1991.

- I let go of the need for approval (as you await someone's acceptance of you).

- I accept risk and remain safe.

- I am strong *and* vulnerable in relationships.

- I show my softness and am thereby powerful.

- I let go of control and am powerful.

- I care about results and let go of the need for results.

- I let go of effort and all that I need comes to me.

- I drop seeking and have all I need.

- I honor my own boundaries and go beyond my limitations.

Simony means attempting to obtain spiritual riches with money. Affirmations are sometimes used in this way. They are powerful spiritual tools that the psyche uses respectfully on its path to higher consciousness. They work because the time has come for a shift to occur. They represent the moment of synchronicity: meaningful coincidence of accessible powers and eased results. To use them for material gain or even for psychic gain or spiritual gain is spiritual materialism. They are not meant to further acquisition. They are meant to encourage and support changes, to collaborate with destiny, to help things unfold as they need to and are ready to. The best attitude with affirmations is one that listens and respects where the psyche wants to take us—not where our ego wants to armor us. Affirmations are the words of surrender to what next will bloom—not the words of grasping what next will aggrandize or profit us.

Beware of the inner critic who floods us with *negations,*

the opposite of affirmations. Design affirmations now that reverse these negations. Use the approach of aikido again: turn back the negative energy against itself without aggression and in such a way that you are empowered:

• If your negation is, "I can't," then affirm "I am." Notice in an affirmation we go all the way. We do not go to "I can," the next step; we go to the final step: "I am." An affirmation must always be a "go for the gold" enterprise.

• If the negation, "That's how I am," becomes "I do it in a whole new way," it cultivates a capacity for a radical reversal of stuckness.

• The negation "I'm guilty" becomes "I acknowledge my responsibility and make amends," if the guilt is appropriate. Or, if it is inappropriate, it becomes "I let go of guilt and make choices with confidence."

Re-frame every negating thought, every self-effacing belief, every diminishing judgment to an affirmation. Remember that our self-images identify our powers: they can expand or contract them.

Your inner self is whole and jumps to attention when it notices you affirming yourself either verbally or by image, as well by actuality. (These are all of equal impact in the unconscious.) This is why imaging works so well in sports. To the unconscious, the image of capacity for winning is equal to an actual capacity for winning.

Our self-portrayals can be freed by affirmations from paralysis into psychic mobility. Affirmations always mean going on, becoming more, growing in self-esteem and releasing our imprisoned powers for their destiny: to let love's light come through.

Conclusion:
When Fight Meets Light

This story is based on a fable from the film, The Doctor, *about a man who was cold and unloving but then became warm and open. Other people, however, still did not trust him because they were so used to his old ways. At first, people may not believe one's transformation from being fearful and hostile to becoming loving and welcoming. It takes a while for an about-face to become a trusted face.*

Farmer Francis could not be fully happy with his plentiful crops. Each day a swarm of crows attacked them with greedy beaks and triumphant squawks. Buds, blossoms, seeds, and fruits were disappearing as fast as they were appearing. In such a crisis, the reclusive Farmer Francis looked only to his bible of answers to life's perplexities: the yellow pages. He looked under the heading "Crop Profits, Protection of" and there found the name "Pontius Poison, the Profiteers' Pal." Farmer Francis' hopes that day were as high as the crow flies as he emerged from Pontius Poison's with all manner of spray, pellet, powder, bomb, chlorinated hydrocarbon, chemosterilant, anthelmintic, and avicide of every toxic potency yet developed by the cunning of man against beast.

The next morning, when Cornelius Crow and his 2000 fine feathered friends flew in for their usual breakfast, all was in readiness for the pogrom. Farmer Francis chuckled, and clicked his heels to see the raiders of his cornucopia fall from left to right, choking and gasping—each with a keen sense of betrayal. The crows had always believed, you see, that the crops had been planted just for them!

Old Cornelius Crow knew better, of course. He had lived through many man-made attempts to curb the population of his clan in the course of his long years as head crow. When he was a mere fledging in another county he had watched helplessly as his parents perished at the hands of an electrified scarecrow. That image burned still in his memory with terror and horror. Meanwhile, he knew that his flock would soon build an immunity to the poisons scattered by Farmer Francis. And so it happened. Soon only 1700 crows scourged the green lands, but not a single one susceptible any longer to even the most virulent product of Pontius Poison, the Profiteers' Pal.

In the face of such a shocking recrudescence of the plague, the hard-hearted Pharaoh in Farmer Francis took refuge once again in the Golden Half of the phone book. (He did not know anyone in the other half.) This time he turned to the section "Pests, Abatement of" and found "Trapper Titus, Interrupter of Natural Processes." Both men beamed with pleasure as they sorted through the many types of traps that could catch a claw, clip a wing, or otherwise cut short the accursed careers of crows.

For the next three days, the snapping, crackling, and popping of traps all over the farm played a symphony of Farmer Francis' version of harmony. At last, he had thwarted the nefarious purposes of his tormentors, those pterodactyls in his private sky.

Meanwhile, with his bird's eye view of the new peril, Cornelius Crow feverishly taught his diminishing crew how to elude the traps and still help themselves to the flourishing grains and fruits of their outdoor smorgasbord. Soon, every bird was adroit at avoiding the traps of "Trapper Titus, Interrupter of Natural Processes." Now 1500 crows feasted happily in this orchestra pit of nurturance, the flat caws of contented crows replacing the sharp snaps of useless traps!

Farmer Francis sought for a solution once again in the

Book of books. Grumbling in wizened frustration, he disregarded such entries as: "Bird Watching—Bird Psychologists—Bird Recipes—Bird Mating—Bird Cemeteries—Bird Catching—Bird Cages—Bird Boarding—" and headed straight to the top of the list: "Bird Annihilation."

"Predatory Puck, Fighting Nature with Nature, since 1995" gleefully pointed out to his new customer that synchronicity certainly was at work! Only today he had received an order of hungry ocelots, large barely tamable cats, who loved to catch, claw, and consume every bird within jumping distance.

And jump they did—all over the fields—until Cornelius Crow instructed his birds of a feather simply to wait until the wheat and corn were higher than the ocelots could jump. And that was exactly what they did. Soon 1400 crows were blithely topping off the crops, and aiming their droppings at the angrily pacing ocelots—now out of prey and out of a job!

Chagrined and defeated, Farmer Francis sat at home enveloped in a miasma of depression. He was now realizing—more keenly than ever—how *alone* he was in this battle and in his life. A long-standing connection between feelings and hands let his fingers do the walking one more time.

La Forza del Destino now enters our story in earnest. Under the listing "Human Isolation, Reversal of," Farmer Francis saw a program for singles called "How To Become Birds of a Feather." In fact, the meeting was to take place that very night. Cranking up his cranky but loyal '59 Chevy truck, he drove the 275 miles from Watsonville to Santa Barbara.

Once arrived, however, he found it impossible to concentrate on the lecture or even to notice the many attractive and available ladies seated around him in the auditorium. But amazing grace was with Farmer Francis that night because he did hear—with full and rapt attention—one sentence of the talk:

"Just stand there with your arms outstretched and with a look of welcome."

Farmer Francis heard and felt these words resound deep within his very soul. This was the Zen blow that now stunned his superficial, fixated existence. And from some never before accessed region of his truly loving but walled-up heart, he realized in one single instant of life—reversing enlightenment—that he did not have to *kill* the birds; he could *live* with them.

Unaware of the longing glances and "come hither" stares directed at him from many women in the audience, unaware of the many ads that would fruitlessly appear the next week in "The Personals" seeking assignations with "the handsome stranger in coveralls at Friday's lecture," unaware of the poem that ended the lecture in which the Ancient Mariner finds the exquisite grace to love the sea monsters, Farmer Francis drove home slowly and then sat silently in deep meditation in his living room for the next three days. Oh what layers of pain and clinging fell away from his armored musculature! Oh what commitments to duality and profit avalanched from the mountains of his mind!

Early that next Tuesday morning, a reborn Francis, full of unconditional love for every creature, danced out in the dawn's luminous glow and stood in his wrinkled clothes, with his arms stretched wide and his whole body shivering in electric anticipation, to welcome his brothers, the birds. But no birds appeared, not that day, nor the next day, nor the next. Francis wondered why not one crow came to accept his sincere offer of love.

Actually, unbeknownst to Francis, Cornelius Crow *had* flown over on a scouting mission that first day. Coming from behind and so unnoticed by Francis, he had halted in midflight and backed up his flurried, frightened feathers as he spied the figure standing in the center of his world. Suddenly every cell in Cornelius' body had shuddered with panic. He was reliving the frightful death of his parents, the abrupt ending of the attention, acceptance, allowing, and affection that had so far sustained his young life.

"Aha," he sobbed as he reversed his direction, "Those old clothes, those open arms could only mean the return of the dreaded electrified scarecrow!" And gathering his companions, away he flew.

CDs and TAPES by David Richo

Dr. Richo gives classes and retreats,
which are often taped.
For a catalog, please send
a legal-sized, self-addressed,
stamped envelope to:

Box 31027
Santa Barbara, CA
93130

Visit his Web site to order online or
to find out about workshops:
www.davericho.com

HOW TO BE AN ADULT

A Handbook on Psychological and Spiritual Integration

by David Richo

(formerly titled: *Letting the Light Through*)

David Richo states that happy, mature people are able to feel and express unconditional love, and have somehow picked up the knack of being generous with their sympathies while still taking care of themselves. How does one do this? In this self-help handbook, he tells us how, based on his many years' experience as a psychologist and workshop leader.

The author uses as a model the heroic journey, three phases of which—departure, struggle, and return—are a model for what happens in us as we evolve from the neurotic ego through a healthy ego to the spiritual Self. Departure is explored by helping the reader deal with fear, anger, and guilt, and build self-esteem. Through struggle one learns to maintain boundaries and build intimacy in relationships. The result is a return to wholeness and love through integration, especially of our shadow side.

Dr. Richo has included checklists and excerpts from literature for meditation in this thoughtful, highly condensed book that is meant to be read and digested little by little for the best results. Here is a positive, inspirational work that will help codependents, addicts, people in relationships—anyone looking to achieve emotional and spiritual health.

Available at local bookstores or order from:

Paulist Press
997 Macarthur Blvd.,
Mahwah, N.J. 07430
www.paulistpress.com

Also available on audiocassette

Also by David Richo
from Paulist Press

The Sacred Heart of the World:
Restoring Mystical Devotion to Our Spiritual Life